W9-BCI-735

Nazism

Issues in Contemporary Civilization

TRANSACTION ISSUES

IN CONTEMPORARY CIVILIZATION

Nazism

A Historical and Comparative Analysis of National Socialism

George L. Mosse

An interview with
Michael A. Ledeen

Transaction Books
New Brunswick, New Jersey

Library of Congress Catalog Number: 77-80873
ISBN: 0-87855-236-7 (cloth) 0-87855-661-3 (paper)
Printed in the United States of America

First Italian-language edition, *Intervista sul nazismo*.
Rome and Bari: Gius. Laterza & Figli, 1977.

Library of Congress Cataloging in Publication Data
Mosse, George Lachmann. Nazism.
    (Issues in contemporary civilization)
    Translation of Intervista sul nazismo.

    1. National socialism. I. Ledeen Michael Arthur,
    1941-   II. Title
    DD256.5.M5713   320.5'33   77-80873
    ISBN 0-87855-236-7
    ISBN 0-87855-661-3 pbk.

2-22-79

Contents

Introduction

It is a pleasure to present this conversation with George L. Mosse to an English-speaking audience. Through one of those peculiarities which now characterize academic endeavor, this was originally published in Italian some two years ago, and now appears in its original version for the first time (the conversation — in English — took place in Rome at the beginning of 1976 and appeared under the title *Intervista sul Nazismo*).

George Mosse has been working on nazism in a systematic way for more than fifteen years, and his several volumes and articles have helped redefine the discussion and analysis of the Third Reich and mass politics in general. From the outset, Mosse challenged two basic tenents of conventional wisdom: first, that Hitler's Germany was a tour de force of propaganda and mass manipulation (aided, perhaps, by economic malaise); and second, that Hitler was the culmination of German history since the Reformation. The first idea — elaborated in such popular works as William Shirer's *Rise and Fall of the Third Reich* — simply explained away the existence of national socialism by focusing on the brilliant manipulative techniques of

the likes of Hitler, Goebbels, and Leni Riefenstahl (or
by offering a combination of this with the notion that
the depression created nazism); the heart of numerous
books of the "From Luther to Hitler" variety explained
away national socialism by arguing that Germans had
always had such tendencies, and that Hitler was simply
a "higher (or lower) form" of well-established German
characteristics. Mosse responded to these stereotypes
by observing that national socialism was a mass movement, and as such could not be explained on the basis
of the propagandistic skill of Nazi leaders unless one
had an extremely dim view of human nature. He insisted that the sources of Hitler's success had to be
discovered in the fabric of German social and cultural
history, and not merely in the machinations of the
leadership. This historical investigation could not resort to the facile generalizations and oversimplifications of the "From Luther to Hitler" school, for Mosse
argued that one had to examine ideas in their historical context and not abstractly. He therefore began his
series of books on national socialism by looking at the
cultural history of Germany in the nineteenth and
twentieth centuries to see the development of those
cultural stereotypes which eventually came to define
popular thought following World War I. In so doing,
he challenged yet another commonplace of cultural
history, the view that ideas were the property of intellectuals, elaborated and discussed by scholars and
first-class thinkers, and restricted to a tiny national
elite. Mosse was primarily interested in the effect of
ideas upon the literate but not necessarily intellectual
public, and insisted that the cultural historian must
deal with this broad and politically powerful popular
culture, and leave the first-class thinkers (who were
rarely understood by the general public) alone. Thus,
for example, Mosse was far more concerned with the
popular view of Nietzsche than with the philosopher's
ideas themselves.

The results of this analysis were very useful. Mosse was able to show that a substantial popular consensus had emerged by the eve of World War I, which had established certain ground rules for the debate which followed. While this consensus was not political in the traditional sense of the term, it would eventually come to define the political debates of the Weimar period in an insidious and eventually fatal way. Paramount among the concepts established by the cultural evolution of Germany in the nineteenth century was that of the *volk,* a word which literally means "people," but which in context took on all sorts of additional shadings and significance. For the Germans of the late nineteenth and early twentieth century, *volk* referred not only to the basic German stock, but also to its history and native landscape, which was viewed as imbued with transcendental values. The volk thus fused spiritual and material elements, and took on an almost religious quality for some nineteenth century thinkers.

The world was divided up into various volks, each with its traditional landscape, history, and physical characteristics. The most dramatic contrast between such groups was that between Germans and Jews. The German volk — according to volkish thinkers — was rooted in the dark and mysterious forests and misty fields of the countryside, and the Germanic soul therefore strove towards the sun. The Jew, in stark contrast, came from the desert, and therefore had an arid and uncreative soul. In one of those remarkable logically contradictory leaps which have characterized human thought, the volkish maintained that urbanism, with all of its attendant disruption of traditional rhythms of life and family structures, was the creation of this desert people. Hence the problems of modernity, which the volkish saw in terms of the stifling of the human spirit, the rise of materialism, and the denigration of true values, were explained as the triumph of a foreign volk on German soil.

Many analysts of German history have noted these themes, but for the most part they have been treated as part of an ongoing tradition of antisemitism and German chauvinism which dates back at least to Martin Luther, if not to the Middle Ages. Mosse rejects such formulas, arguing instead that volkish thought must be granted a certain integrity of its own, and that it must be viewed as part of the search for German identity which characterized the period from the Napoleonic Wars to the triumph of Hitler. Volkish thought was invariably nationalistic and condemned Jewish influence in Germany, but it was not necessarily antisemitic. Many volkish thinkers believed that the Jews had made a unique contribution to human history, and that they might do so again in the future, but they felt that the Jews simply belonged in their own native landscape rather than in Western Europe. Not surprisingly, a significant strand of Zionism accepted this very analysis in order to urge their coreligionaries to leave Europe for Palestine.

Furthermore, volkish thought, insidious as it was, did not take the vicious and ultimately homicidal turn of racism in the twentieth century. And both volkish and racist thinkers were quite different from the antisemites of the Reformation period. Mosse argues that any attempt to establish a continuum between Lutheran and Nazi antisemitism is extremely dangerous, both because racism of the Nazi period had an entirely different theoretical underpinning, and because the historical context was changed. Lutheranism's hatred of Jews rested on religious arguments, and not on a pseudobiological racism. For a Lutheran, Jews could save themselves by conversion and baptism, but no such escape hatch existed for Jews under Nazism. Moreover, the mass movement which Hitler captured for his own purposes saw the Jew as the symbol of a corrupt modernity which threatened to submerge the true Aryan in a sea of materialism, while the religious antisemites of the past viewed Jews as the enemy of revelation and true faith. In other words, ideas themselves are not determinant; the historian must deal with ideas and passions *in context.*

This is not to say that Mosse's analysis does not deal with the importance of religious tradition in Germany, but it does not rest upon the superficial similarities between certain phases of the Reformation and national socialism. Mosse rejects the traditional approach adopted by students of the history of ideas, and this is the reason for his long and detailed study of the nature of the mass movement which laid the groundwork for Hitler's success, a study which found its culmination in *The Nationalization of the Masses.*

Volkish thought penetrated virtually all segments of German society, from one end of the political spectrum to the other, and from the upper to the lower classes. But there is a great distance from the frequently incoherent and vaguely defined volkish ideology to the formation of the Third Reich, and Mosse — rare among contemporary historians — has attempted to find the missing link through an investigation of the rise of the mass movement of the German Right which he calls the "new politics." This mass movement was far more than a group of people subscribing in varying degrees to a set of ideas; it was a new form of political activity, which grew up around the search for German unification. In the end, the new politics became the vehicle for the triumph of Adolf Hitler, but over the course of more than a century, it enlisted the passionate participation of a great multitude of Germans with differing political allegiances.

The New Politics

> We have been concerned with a cultural phenomenon
> which cannot be subsumed under the traditional canons
> of political theory. For it was not constructed as a logical
> or coherent system that could be understood through a
> rational analysis of philosophical writings. The
> phenomenon which has been our concern was a secular
> religion, the continuation from primitive and Christian
> times of viewing the world through myth and symbol,
> acting out one's hopes and fears within ceremonial and
> liturgical forms.
> The new politics filled Germany with national monu-
> ments and public festivals, the objectifications of con-
> scious and unconscious wishes in which millions found a
> home.

Those who are used to hearing that religion was
separated from politics in the modern era in the same
way that church and state are separated in many modern constitutions may marvel at these words, but they
lie at the heart of George Mosse's view of the modern
period. It is hardly surprising that an historian who
spent much of his career studying the religious elements in political philosophy should become intrigued
by the religious themes in modern mass movements,
and some of the most fascinating and insightful passages in the conversation that follows are dedicated to
this subject. Here again, Mosse has gone in the face of
conventional wisdom, which would have us discuss
politics and religion in separate and neatly organized
compartments, as if religion were set aside for
weekend observance when political activity was sus-
pended. In real life the two are closely intermingled, to
a far greater extent than most scholars seem to be
aware, and Mosse — who made his mark as a young
man by pointing out the religious basis for Enlighten-

ment political thought — is acutely sensitive to their interpenetration.

In keeping with his insistence that Hitler's ideas be discussed in the context of the industrial age, Mosse argues that traditional religion lost its grasp on the populace with the massive demographic changes of the late eighteenth and early nineteenth centuries, and that people found themselves increasingly confused and alienated from their own society. In an ultimately successful attempt to restore the wholeness of the human experience, various practitioners of the new politics developed ideas, ceremonies, and other forms of group experience that brought people together in a new kind of association. Whether it be the German Youth Movement of the late nineteenth century or the picturesque gymnastic association of Father Jahn which followed the Napoleonic conquest of Germany, all of these quasi-religious, often mystical and irrational groups had a single yearning in common: the quest for a sense of belonging based on a passionate conviction that the universe was intrinsically meaningful, and that Germany would have an heroic role to play in it.

This search for belonging generally took the form of a quest for the creation of a new community, and went hand in hand with a growing belief that modern society had lost touch with the basic needs of mankind. While the new politics stressed the creativity and spontaneity of the human race, the new cities and the relentless advance of industry appeared to crush originality, impose a grey and monotonous conformity, and destroy any hope of contact with nature itself. This contrast between the presumed spontaneity, genuineness, and creativity of mankind and the sterility and gloom imposed by the advance of the industrial age was accompanied by widespread acceptance of the stereotype of the Jew, who served as the incarnation of all that had gone wrong. The Jew was a city creature, devoid of creativity and spontaneity, typically a middleman who traded in other's products, given over to the quest for material gain with no interest in or capacity for the more spiritual aspects of life.

While this stereotype might bear a superficial similarity to that of the antisemites of the late Reformation and early modern period, it belonged uniquely to the industrial age. As Mosse observes, the German Revolution hinged on antisemitism in the sense that the Jew became the symbol of everything which had gone wrong with the modern world. But it is important to stress that the symbol of the Jew was effective because it stood in marked contrast to a dynamic idea of human nature and of the human community. The German Revolution had a positive goal in mind, albeit a terribly vague and even irrational one, and the dynamic of the revolutionary mass movement was heightened and focused by the counterpoint of the Jew.

The German Revolution

The center of the German Revolution was of course nationalism, emerging from the humiliation of the Napoleonic Wars (called "wars of national liberation" in Germany) and developing throughout the following century. It has become a commonplace to observe that German nationalism, like that in Italy, was rather more virulent than the French or British varieties because it was born relatively late and because for a long time Germany was simply a geographic expression or a vision of the faithful. Throughout the nineteenth century, expectations surrounding German unification grew, until the phenomenon took on an almost messianic aspect. These great expectations were not realized by the creation of the Wilhelminian State, and even Bismarck's revenge in 1870 did not sate the appe-

tite of those who expected the new Germany to transform the course of all human history. The defeat of
the Great War only exacerbated the situation, and
gave the enemies of Weimar a ready-made weapon in
the postwar years.

Yet Hitler's success was not merely the result of
German frustration and hatred of the Jews, for the
preceding century had seen the rise of a new kind of
liturgy which effectively mobilized masses of Germans
in national rituals and ceremonies which gave a new
sense of meaning and belonging to the participants. In
Mosse's view, the great ceremonies of the Third Reich
like the famous Nuremberg rallies immortalized in
Leni Riefenstahl's film *The Triumph of the Will* were
simply a grandiose form of liturgical ceremonies
which had been developed by both Left and Right in
the nineteenth century. In the conversation which follows, some of the most illuminating passages deal with
the question of ritual and liturgy, and Mosse compares
the ceremonies of the Third Reich with those of the
baroque age, when the forces of the Counterreforma-
tion reenlisted the allegiance of Christian Europe
through the use of new ceremonial forms and glorious
celebrations. The comparison may seem shocking to
many, but Mosse insists that the success of the new
politics was due in large part to a recognition that men
and women in the nineteenth and twentieth centuries,
just like their predecessors in the seventeenth century,
desperately searched for meaning through collective
participation, and that Hitler realized that a successful
mass movement had to be based on this quest for
spiritual fulfillment. The forms of such a mass movement were unique to the historical context, but the
necessity for liturgy and ceremony is viewed as a constant in human history. What is so striking about
Mosse's treatment is that it is not simply an extrapola-
tion from anthropology to history (although he spent

considerable time studying anthropological works before writing *The Nationalization of the Masses).* Mosse's
analysis rests upon a great body of original research
into the specific forms the new politics took throughout the nineteenth and early twentieth centuries in
Germany. The result is an original blending of new
information with insights from a variety of scholarly
disciplines.

In the course of his research, Mosse occasionally
looked at some non-German examples of the new politics: a French trade-union movement, and the case of
Gabrielle D'Annunzio, the eccentric Italian poet who
became a hero of World War I and then occupied the
city of Fiume for sixteen months at the end of the war.
In both cases, Mosse found a similar quest for meaning
and a similar combination of political and religious
themes. I have argued elsewhere that D'Annunzio's
attempt to create the "Free State of Fiume" represented the first full-blown attempt in this century to
organize a government in Western Europe around
this new kind of ceremonial politics, and that it was in
many ways a great success. As Mosse himself has stated
on several occasions, one should beware of transpos-
ing historical models from one country to another,
even when they both belong to Western Europe, but it
is significant that such forms should have grown up in
the two countries which arrived last at national unification in Western Europe, and which had developed
messianic expectations about the effects of unification.
It is also significant that these were the countries which
gave the word *fascism* to the Western political vocabulary.

The Problem of Fascism

The question of fascism as a general European
phenomenon understandably receives extended

treatment in this conversation, for Mosse is convinced that it is possible to deal with fascism as a European-wide revolution of the Right. He is of the opinion that fascism represented a search for a "third way" between capitalism and communism, which would liberate human beings from the alienation of industrial society and still guarantee them individual fulfillment. As one would expect, Mosse insists that the festivals of fascism played a major role in creating the illusion of fulfillment, and that the extension of politics into every area of human endeavor—the essence of what used to be called "totalitarianism" — meant that citizens had a constant sense of participation in the "cause."

Mosse recognizes the significant differences between the various European fascisms, and also admits that there were elements of some fascist movements which were decidedly left-wing. It might be objected by some that this vitiates the attempt to establish a general model for European fascism, but Mosse insists that there were sufficient similarities to warrant the use of the term as a general one. It is unlikely that this slim volume will resolve the debate, but the problems raised here help to define the problem. It is clear— both from what Mosse says, and from an earlier discussion of fascism with Renzo De Felice*—that the old model of fascism has broken down. It used to be a commonplace that Hitler and Mussolini were the two great exemplars of a monolithic movement (which at times was extended to Japan and Brazil), but this monolith is no longer acceptable to scholars. Even if one agrees with Mosse that there were basic impulses common to all fascisms, it is still clear that there were profound differences between German national socialism and Italian fascism.

*Renzo De Felice, *Fascism: An Informal Introduction to Its Theory and Practice*. An Interview with Michael A. Ledeen (New Brunswick, N.J.: Transaction Books, 1976).

The common impulse running through fascist movements was disgust with liberal democracy and rejection of parliamentary governments. Whether this took the form of Mussolini's ephemeral corporate state or the more ambitious projects of Goering and Speer, all fascists were convinced that liberalism was incapable of meeting the challenges of the twentieth century, that the new nations of Western Europe needed charismatic leadership, and that the people had to be mobilized in a great national effort to over-come the obstacles to self-fulfillment and national greatness which had developed over the course of the preceding century. This inevitably meant dictatorship, although Mosse rightly stresses that the fascists them-selves viewed their governments as a "higher form" of true democracy. Hitler was a primus inter pares, and Mussolini frequently spoke of himself and his regime as the true expression of the desires of the Italian people.

Mosse rightly condemns several attempts to over-simplify the question of fascism, pointing out that the traditional liberal explanation—that fascism was some sort of temporary aberration—does not explain the great success of fascism everywhere in Europe, or that it finally fell only because of military defeat. Liberals who wish to believe that fascism was simply imposed on Europeans have great difficulty in explaining the vir-tual nonexistence of opposition to fascism from within, and they generally ignore the fact that fascism came to power by legitimate means, not via coups d'etat. As for the Marxist explanations—fascism as the creature of monopoly capitalism—Mosse points out that they fail for lack of evidence. The success of Hitler was not due to covert financing from German industrialists and militarists; if anything, it was the latter who were manipulated by the Nazis. Hence, more recent Marxist studies have been looking for different models, albeit

with the same lack of success as their ideological pre-
cursors.

Methodology

Another interesting aspect of this conversation with
George Mosse is his insistence upon a dialectical approach to historical problems. Mosse's point is altogether legitimate, although perhaps the terminol-
ogy is not altogether felicitous. For too many years,
scholars from various disciplines have divided reality
into various compartments, roughly corresponding to
the departments in modern universities (a practice
which John Hexter has termed "tunnel theories" of
reality). Thus each department gets its own "factor":
sociologists get the social factor, economists the
economic factor, psychologists the psychological factor, and so forth. Ideas are either dealt with by
philosophers (there is still no department of ideology,
although "historians of ideas" made a run at this for a
time) or treated as curiosities by sociologists and
historians. For the most part, the relationship between
people's ideas and their political behavior has remained one of the least analyzed problems in both
contemporary politics and historical scholarship. Yet
this, as Mosse points out, is one of the most important
of all questions, and it will neither go away nor be
revolved by "quantification." Somehow the dynamic
interrelationship between people's ideas and the social
and political reality in which these ideas function must
be dealt with. It may be George Mosse's greatest contribution to have attempted to deal with this problem
in a clear and useful way.

For Mosse, the first obligation of the cultural historian is to establish the true content of popular culture.
This task is not a particularly fascinating one, for intellectuals prefer to deal with first-class thinkers rather

than popularizers. It is more interesting to read Freud than to wade through attempts to explain psychoanalysis in weekly and monthly magazines. But the popular press, best sellers, radio programs, and the cinema are of far greater political importance than the writings of great men and women, and the cultural historian must start with the former. Then, it is necessary to determine the context in which these ideas exist, for the easiest of all errors is that of dealing with the ideas themselves rather than their particular historical content. One must avoid facile mistakes such as presuming that certain words always mean the same thing (*democracy*, for example, has an astonishingly large number of definitions in the modern period), or assuming that ideas are not altered dramatically by national differences. Finally, one must attempt to re-create reality from the inside out, "getting inside the heads" of the historical actors. Then, and only then, can a true historical (or contemporary) analysis be undertaken. To his great credit, George Mosse has performed such an analysis. One may quibble here or there with his conclusions, but all of us owe him a great debt. He is one of the first historians to deal with Nazism as a mass movement, owing its success to the participation and active support of the majority of the German people. He has refused the easy explanations, and insisted on a historical analysis which is exceedingly difficult and frequently morally repulsive. Yet, as he observes, it is absolutely necessary. For to write the history of fascism is to write the history of the failure of freedom in modern times in Western Europe. If those of us who cherish human freedom expect to be able to defend it, we must understand how it came to be destroyed just a generation or two ago.

Michael A. Ledeen

Chapter One

Ledeen: For someone who works on national socialism, your biography is of particular interest, wouldn't you say?

Mosse: Perhaps, but I was very young when I left Germany and never experienced national socialism.

Ledeen: You have no personal recollections?

Mosse: Not really. I was fifteen when I left boarding school — which was not national socialist but was infiltrated by national socialism — but I simply do not recall any pressure or any of the events that went on. For one thing, I was in the country. For another, when the family had to leave in January 1933, I was delighted to go to Paris. I had never been to Paris before, so my first visit to Paris, as is natural for a young boy, blanked out all greater world affairs. It was an adventure. I had always heard about Paris since my family had been instrumental in furthering German-French friendships ever since World War I.

Ledeen: I think it might be useful to say something

about your family, which was one of the leading German-Jewish families prior to Hitler.

Mosse: My grandfather on my mother' side founded one of the largest publishing houses in the country. First he modernized advertising in Germany, and then he founded newspapers like the *Berliner Tageblatt.* The business included a worldwide advertising agency as well as a major liberal newspaper publishing house.

Ledeen: And your father was the head of the publishing house?

Mosse: Yes. It was owned by the family. At that time prestigious but not really so influential German newspapers like the *Berliner Tageblatt* and the *Frankfurter Zeitung* were owned by families.

Ledeen: You left rather early with your family, didn't you?

Mosse: We had to leave. The other big Jewish newspaper family in Berlin, the Ullsteins[1], stayed a little longer but the *Berliner Tageblatt* and the popular *Volkszeitung,* which was another one of my father's papers, were always hated by the Nazis in a special manner. So we had no choice, luckily enough. Leaving was more complicated for my father because Goering summoned him back in March under the threat that if he did not return, reprisals would be taken against the Jewish employees of the firm. Goering probably offered my father "Aryanization"[2] for himself and the family. This policy barely existed, but you know the chief of the German Air Force provided one example. My father refused and was supposed to be murdered in the famous Blue Train en route from Berlin to Paris. But it did not come off. I think the reason

Goering wanted to Aryanize my father was that the Europeanwide Mosse advertising agency could have made an excellent spy cover. Also the name "Mosse" was useful for the regime. For example, I have some unpublished correspondence between Goebbels and the chief editor of the *Berliner Tageblatt*, Theodor Wolff, in which Goebbels asked Wolff to come back and take over again because the Nazis wanted to have this front of respectability. After all, the Mosse publishing house was well known outside Germany. It stood for something, and if the Nazis could annex that, it would be useful for them, at least for a while.

Ledeen: We're talking about January 1933. What became of George Mosse after 1933?

Mosse: Well, I managed to get out only because of the German penchant for order. I don't remember the exact date but there was a new law pending according to which one had to have an exit visa. I left in a ferry across the Lake of Constance fifteen minutes before midnight, when the law was to go into effect. But instead of stopping me, the SA guards[3], knowing perfectly well who I was, let me go since the law did not take effect for another quarter of an hour. That is really what I owe my life to because I remember them looking at each other and raising their eyebrows when I went to give my passport.

Ledeen: And from there you went to Paris?

Mosse: Then to Paris and then to school in England. A school called Bootham School in York which had produced a great many historians, such as A.J.P. Taylor. The school had a superb history master, Mr. Leslie Gilbert, who trained a generation of historians in England and who got me interested in history.

Ledeen: And you stayed in England until after the war?

Mosse: No, until 1939. I left the school in 1937 and then went to Cambridge. I did very badly in my Cambridge entrance because I never had any mathematics, but in my day you could flunk a field three times, and eventually I was admitted to Downing College. I entered Cambridge in 1937 and stayed for two years studying history.

Ledeen: Medieval history, modern history?

Mosse: Modern history then did not exist in the way we now teach it. One must not forget that modern history in England and on the continent ended with the seventeenth and eighteenth centuries. Nothing beyond that was really taught at Cambridge in any meaningful fashion. So everybody was perforce a medievalist and early modernist.

Ledeen: With whom did you work at Cambridge?

Mosse: The greatest influence on me was a man whose *History of England* my history master gave me to read at school: namely George Macauley Trevelyan.[4] Today there is a lot of criticism of this great Whig historian and his *History of England,* but for a boy my age it was a revelation. Unfortunately, Trevelyan was probably the worst lecturer I have ever known. In fact, he read his proofs during lecture. So he started his lecture with four hundred students and finished with four, of whom I was one. But it was Trevelyan who really introduced me to history together with Helen Maude Cam, in whose seminar I spent four entire months on the deposition of Richard II. Later in the fifties Helen Cam went on to become the first woman professor at Harvard. She was an eminent medievalist.

Then I must add a third historian who today is almost forgotten. He was called Lord Bernard Manning. He was not a lord, that was his first name. He taught us medieval history, very well indeed I thought. I never really had great luck with my tutors. Anyhow in Cambridge I wasn't a very serious student. You know, in those days before democratization, one worked during the vacations and not in term. Term was a round of breakfasts, teas, and parties. So I didn't do very well in the first examinations which were the only ones I took. I only got a second, which isn't very good. The upshot, of course, of all of this was that I didn't work as hard as I should have and that I never had any formal training in modern history, which became my chief interest in the 1960s.

Ledeen: From England, then, you moved to the United States?

Mosse: Not exactly, I came to America because my father was emigrating in August 1939. But I was supposed to go back. I had a reentry permit to England in September when the war broke out, and I was stranded. Something had to be done. I had been to a Quaker school in England. I knew nothing about America, but I knew there was a Quaker city called Philadelphia. So I took a train to Philadelphia, asked a taxi driver to drive me to the first Quaker institution which was Friends' Select School. They told me they had two colleges — neither of which I had heard of — Haverford and Swarthmore. The Haverford train went first and President William Wistar Comfort of Haverford, who still talked in the Quaker manner, said, "We will take thee at once." I didn't have any money either. And that was really luck, great luck, because at Haverford there were then two men who really taught me all I know about historical research.

One was a Shakespearean scholar, Leslie Hotson, one of the great detectives. He found out who killed Christopher Marlowe. He found out how Shakespeare made out his last will and testament. And the other was William Lunt, who was the professor of history and one of the leading medievalists of his time. Between them they taught me how to go about historical investigation. I was Hotson's assistant and I did my honors paper under William Lunt.

Ledeen: Did you get a degree?

Mosse: I got a B.S. with honors. I then went to Harvard to graduate school in medieval history under a really great teacher, perhaps the greatest teacher that I've ever known — Charles Howard McIlwain — an authority on English constitutional history. I did my doctorate with him on a subject which became my first book. It was already concerned with power and the state and was called *The Struggle for Sovereignty in England.*

Ledeen: How is it that starting from medieval constitutional law you arrived finally at the twentieth century? You've come at it almost century by century, haven't you? Books on the sixteenth century, then the seventeenth century, articles on the Enlightenment, then books on the nineteenth century and then finally . . .

Mosse: Well, it really isn't quite that simple. My first book was on the seventeenth century, and I have kept this early modern interest up to a certain degree because my last book on this subject, *Europe in the 16th Century* with Helmut Koenigsberger, was published in 1968.[5] But the way I came to modern history was again a matter of circumstances. I've always believed one should be interested in problems and not chronology, and so the problems I have worked on — the problem of the relationship between reason and irrationalism, the problem of Reason of State — which occupied most of my work in the earlier centuries, aren't so far removed from the problems I worked on later. But the shift in centuries came about concretely, since after my first position at the University of Iowa I got a call to the University of Wisconsin in 1955 with the proviso that I specialize in the nineteenth and twentieth centuries. That actually started it off. Otherwise, I think I might have gone on in the sixteenth, seventeenth, and eighteenth centuries, for a while longer.

Ledeen: So it was actually the position that was available at the University of Wisconsin that made you turn to contemporary history.

Mosse: Yes, but I also had a certain interest in it. As I said, up to 1961 when my *Culture of Modern Europe* appeared[6], I had dealt exclusively with the earlier centuries. Indeed, I might say I was the last student at Harvard to take examinations for the Ph.D. in the period entirely before 1700. So I really knew very little of the period after 1700. I wrote an article which went into the eighteenth century, but it was on puritanism, which was part of my interest, and casuistry and the Reformation, all matters which occupied me. I must stress again that the problems that I wrote about — the viability of Christianity and how it absorbed ideas of Reason of State and policy — is an eternal problem which doesn't really vary that much from century to century. The theology I worked on was above all concerned with popular piety, and popular piety and modern ideology are not so far removed from each other. Finally, my really passionate interest during the late fifties on which I worked in Rome at the Vatican library — the baroque — is directly relevant to modern mass movements, their theatricality, and all that goes with it. So I wouldn't say that there is a major break. I would say that there is a continuity of interest. Moreover, if I look at the work of my students (and I have had students in all these periods) it comes out very clearly that their concern is with the problem of myth and reality, if you like, between asthetics and politics, or theology and politics. The books of my students reflect very clearly an interest in the myths people live by, their political relevance, and the penetration of these myths by reality.

Ledeen: I'd like to talk a little bit about the intellectual influences on you that you consider particularly important, and also about the problems that you deal with and the kind of methodology that you brought to bear on them. It seems to me that your uniqueness lies both in the problems that you choose and the way that you treat them.

Mosse: I should say that the intellectual influences upon me were not really any of my teachers but three men, of whom I only knew one, and only very fleetingly at that. That is to say, Friedrich Meinecke, the German historian with his idea of power and Reason of State. One of my early efforts was to interest American historians (who were very deficient in theory at that time) in the idea of Reason of State which was an important reality in American political thought, and which had even infected American Puritans. The only article written in appreciation of this effort of mine to bring Meinecke to bear on English and American Puritan theology is by an Italian historian — Professor Georgio Spini. It is very typical that it should be a European who understood what I did rather than an American.

Ledeen: And aside from Meinecke, who were the other major intellectual influences?

Mosse: The second influence on me was Benedetto Croce. I met Croce once for just half an hour, and it was a great experience for me. I was writing the book on casuistry then, called *The Holy Pretence* (1957)[7], which was about how Machiavelli was absorbed into English theology. Croce took a very nice interest in that and, in fact, gave me some very good suggestions. But he influenced me, above all, through his concept of the totality of history, something I believe very much — that outside history there is no reality. In fact, I start one of my books on the Reformation with a quotation from Croce, and *The Holy Pretence* uses as an introduction a Crocean formulation: what is the ideological connection between the Renaissance and the Reformation? I answered, to put it briefly, that the connection is in the reception by divines of Machiavelli; not in secular political thought, but in theology.

Ledeen: And the third influence?

Mosse: The third influence is Johan Huizinga with his idea of myth. The longer I work the more I become convinced that the idea of myth is a very important one, not just for anthropologists but also for historians. The historian's function must be to understand the myths that people live by because these myths very often have a tenuous link to reality, though they are placed within reality.

Now perhaps I should add a fourth influence — my late friend George Lichtheim — because he taught me the Hegelian approach. This came late in my life, not really until the late 1950s, but it has been determinant. That is the insight for example that there is a dialectic between myth and reality, and that all of history must be viewed in a dynamic and dialectical fashion. I consider myself a Hegelian.

Ledeen: This dialectic, as I understand it, is a traditional Hegelian one, is it not? That is, it is not purely a materialistic dialectic, not simply a dialectic between social forces or social classes.

Mosse: It is more materialist than Hegel, because obviously today we cannot be pure Hegelians. We realize, after all, through the important schools of social history, that the dialectic is, in fact, between myth and social forces. I would say between myth and what Marx called objective reality, that is social, political, and economic forces.

Ledeen: Could you elaborate on this a little bit? Could you perhaps make it a bit more specific? Is there some example of the way in which you see this dialectic working?

Mosse: Let us take Hitler, who is, after all, the subject of our talk. Hitler's myths were very strong, but Hitler's success was due to the fact that while his myth — of race, and let us say of the occult, in which he also believed — was detached from reality and gave him his goal, he also had a very strong sense of the objective reality, that is to say he had a profound sense of the political and social forces of his day, of political timing and tactics, and this made reaching the goal possible. Myth and reality worked together in a dialectical fashion. They were interrelated until, with a dictator like Hitler — and here I am saying nothing new — myth eventually won out over the objective forces. At the end he moved troops around that didn't exist, he gave commands that weren't executed, he retired ever more into his dream world, his world of myth and symbol. But to be successful there has to be an interaction.

Let me give you another example. Let us talk about the baroque and modern mass politics. The baroque is full of myth, theater, and symbols which carry you away from the reality of this world. But the very success of the Jesuits was that while carrying you away from this world they really integrated you into their political system. Now this approach is not unique. You have the same thing later in Richard Wagner who believed that his operas would strengthen certain myths by which people live so that through their myths they could enter into existing reality and then transform that reality according to the myths.

Chapter Two

Ledeen: Can we come at this problem from a slightly different direction? Taking your work as a touchstone and focusing on national socialism, I think that we can say that you have analyzed the various elements of this dialectic over the course of the past ten or fifteen years. There was *The Crisis of German Ideology,* [8] which was an elaboration of the content of the myth itself.

Mosse: Exactly.

Ledeen: This was an analysis of the ideology, and you tried to describe how the ideology took form and then how it penetrated various strata of German society.

Mosse: Yes, but this work was also influenced by Croce's dictum that all is history. One reason that I wrote this book was a conviction that you cannot have any successful myth without historical preparation. Just as you cannot invent popular festivals, so you cannot invent myth. I tried, then, to show the roots of this myth, which was then actualized under national socialism.

Ledeen: Indeed, one of the unique elements about your work is that in none of your books have you restricted the analysis to the period which is commonly taken to be that of the rise of national socialism, that is from the very late nineteenth century through the Weimar Republic. You have always taken a much longer view of the question. Indeed, you begin your analysis with the Napoleonic Wars.

Mosse: There is a reason for that. It is not that I believe in the model of what used to be called "from Luther to Hitler." That is a ridiculous proposition. I believe in — again we return to this theme — a certain dialectic between continuities and discontinuities, or, to put it better, between continuities and their activation. There must always be a tradition to be activated. I am convinced that one of the most important events in modern German history is the wars of liberation against Napoleon. This should not astonish anyone; wars of liberation are always the most important event in modern nations, and that is why I go back there. German nationalism — Germans' views of themselves — largely derives from their wars of liberation. Again I must say that this is not astonishing, but it is always misinterpreted. It is interpreted as being a straight line, but there is no straight line; this is simply one view which Germans had of themselves and it became the most important one only after 1918. But until 1918 there were other ways of viewing oneself in Germany: there was a strong liberal movement, there was a strong socialist movement, but if you are talking about national socialism what became important was this particular tradition of the wars of liberation.

Ledeen: Yes, so that in *The Crisis of German Ideology* and in the article on the "Mystical Origins of National

Socialism" in *The Journal of the History of Ideas*[9] you talked about the ideas and the myths themselves. But more recently, and particularly in *The Nationalization of the Masses*[10], you've been talking about the forms which these myths took in social celebrations. This seems to be something quite new and might be said to represent an anthropological approach to history.

Mosse: Yes. It does have a lot to do with anthropology but I see it rather as an attempt to see how these myths were activated and how they were actually brought to the people. Of course, many have read the nationalist literature which I have discussed from time to time. But that is not the whole story, that is the tradition, the myth to be used. The question is, how was it to be used? It wasn't used in a literary form because fascist movements — and not only national socialism — weren't really so wedded to literary forms. The myths were used as part of mass movements. They were part of the symbolism of mass movements. That is why I became interested in that phenomenon after 1918.

There is another problem here worth mentioning. If you examine, as I have, German popular literature — the literature read in the millions before and after 1914 — perhaps you will be surprised to find it liberal, tolerant, philosemitic, etc. So you have to explain why a nation brought up on literature, which is all any liberal could possibly desire, went so wrong. The answer, in my opinion, is that many people believed that they were reading fairy tales and that it took a Hitler to make the fairy tale come true. In other words, there is in all fascism, I believe, and not just in national socialism, a sense that it is a door into a utopia of tolerance, of happiness, of productivity, and all the things that people long for. As far as I know, no fascism (and certainly not national socialism) prided itself on its oppression, but thought instead that its oppression was a transitory state necessary to bring about a kind of utopia.

I should add to this that this utopia was brought before the people in mass movements, ceremonies, and symbols.

Ledeen: Yes. That is the theme of *The Nationalization of the Masses.* You talk about the development of a political style which has, after all, become our political style — the style of the mass movement today, of what the Italians call "the politics of the piazza." All the politics which you described in *The Nationalization of the Masses,* —the development of public festivals, the evolution of political rites which are modeled on old religious rites, the development of sacred themes, sacred symbols, relics, holy spaces — are all the themes with which we have lived in this century. Furthermore, there is an implication in *The Nationalization of the Masses,* if I may develop a marginal theme here for just a second, that these themes are not just unique to national socialism but are, in fact, the model for the modern political world in general. Is that fair, do you think?

Mosse: Well, first of all, it is not unique to national socialism. D'Annunzio can claim a certain priority, except that he wasn't well known in Germany. German development, I think, is really quite independent of this. But we must say that after 1918 there was a great thrust in this direction because it was a time of continuing crisis. But wherever there is not a time of crisis — economic, social or political — I do not think we have the politics of the piazza. Then parliamentary government works and works well, and can, in fact, survive. After 1918 the nations which did not experience revolution, counterrevolution, economic crisis, or near civil war, didn't have this kind of politics. I'm thinking of France, England, Holland. After 1945 when times again were good or stabilized you do not have the politics of the piazza. I would say that that kind of politics goes together with a certain crisis.

Ledeen: And yet in *The Nationalization of the Masses* your theme is the development of this political form through a period of a century which is characterized by ups and downs. There seems to be an almost constant development of political festivals, political myths, political rituals, and so forth.

Mosse: Again, there has to be a tradition in order for anything to happen later. But I never said in the book or meant to say that the vast majority of Germans between 1817 and 1914 were taken up with such myths. There were some, perhaps a great many, but that is all we can say then — only after 1918 does it become generalized.

Ledeen: And this in reaction to the crisis?

Mosse: This is in reaction to the great crisis after the war in Germany. Remember in Germany there is not only revolution and counterrevolution, there is also foreign occupation by the French of the Ruhr Valley.[11] There is inflation. There are all these objective realities which I think are very important. People are disoriented. People want a healthy and happy world. People want to participate in politics and they turn to the politics of the piazza (as you call it) for their participation.

Ledeen: This is really almost a religious phenomenon as you see it, isn't it?

Mosse: Any phenomen of our civilization is in a sense a Christian phenomenon because Christianity is what people know. Any political theology grows quite naturally out of Christian theology — the sacred flame, the sacred spaces. The Nazis even had altars in the factories—little rooms which they called worship rooms which were constructed like churches except that on the altar there were the symbols of the party.

Ledeen: Most people have talked about this phenomenon as anti-Christian, but you see a kind of continuity.

Mosse: That is an undialectical way of thinking if you say it is an anti-Christian phenomenon. It is at the same time Christian and anti-Christian. Political ceremonies were Christian in that they adopted the rhythm and some of the forms of Christianity. The famous dialogue from the balcony by D'Annunzio, Mussolini, and Hitler goes back, of course, to the dialogue, the Responsa, in the Christian liturgy. In fact, for centuries this was the kind of liturgy people used. This is not astonishing. What was anti-Christian was the specific opposition to parts of the Christian belief, to the belief that Christ redeemed all mankind, to the belief that baptism was more important than race, and above all to the powerful organization of the Church. But we must not forget that everywhere at first churches and fascism cooperated, that the churches themselves saw an advantage in fascism. What advantage? That a political faith might reflect on a religious faith, and then the churches would be full again. That didn't happen, of course. But you can see that there is a dialectical relationship without any doubt whatsoever.

Ledeen: Can we elaborate on this just a little bit, on the connection between churches and national socialism? In your book you stress that this is rather more a Protestant phenomenon than a Catholic phenomenon. Is this, in your view, because of the strength of

Catholic liturgy and Catholic ritual?

Mosse: We now come to a German situation. I think in Italy it was not this way. But in Germany the reason is that Protestantism was the religion of the state, that Protestant liturgy ever since the Reformation was confused and therefore all sorts of foreign elements could enter Protestantism. So you had a Germanic Christianity.

I think that Catholicism in Germany was also loyal and had great difficulty in opposing national socialism — but it did so largely because Catholicism had its own political party, its own structure. It was really in a way a state within a state. Therefore it feared the national socialists. An attempt was made to bring them together by Bishop Aloîs Hudal[12] who was the German Catholic bishop in Rome. Bishop Hudal wrote a very famous book on national socialism and Christianity in which he asked the Nazis to stay out of theology and then everything would be fine. Let the Nazis regard themselves as a secular faith and we can collaborate with them. The Vatican, by the way, rejected Hudal's book but still I think it was a very widespread idea. The second matter which is never brought out but which I think is very important in all of this is that if the Catholic bishops and priests had been anti-Nazi after 1933, they would have lost their congregations. It wasn't that easy. There were attempts by certain Catholic priests and bishops to oppose the Nazis, but they soon realized this meant losing their following. So they chose the lesser evil.

Ledeen: But you think that there was more Protestant support for national socialism than there was Catholic, wasn't there?

Mosse: This isn't a matter of speculation. Until 1933

there was Protestant support and very little Catholic support in the densely Catholic regions dominated by the Center party. But eventually even the Center party was inclined to play along with Hitler. Even the Center party voted for the famous Enabling Act[13], which gave Hitler all the power. After 1933 the Catholic church's attitude was much more positive than before 1933. Before 1933 Catholics were not allowed to vote national socialist. That doesn't mean that many didn't do it, but after 1933 there was a firm compromise which was only broken in 1939 by euthanasia, the killing of the incurably sick and insane. The Church was still powerful enough to put an ostensible stop to the use of euthanasia in 1939.

Ledeen: Ostensible?

Mosse: Yes, because euthanasia actually went on. So the Church was by no means devoid of power, and influence.

Ledeen: Now, we've been talking about the origins of national socialism in terms of the development of the political style which you call the new politics and in terms of the development of a certain kind of ideology. It might be worth the trouble for just a minute to take a hard look at the specific forms of this political style, to take a look at the content of this ideology. The first thing to be said about it is that it rested on the idea of race.

Mosse: Well, that's quite true, but I think I would like to put it in slightly different terms. If we speak of ideology apart from the social and other concrete forces I would say that national socialist ideology really rested on two pillars. First on a look backwards and then on a look forward. In other words, it combined in an in-

genious fashion traditionalism with, if you like, modernity — traditionalism with the leap forward. I would
summarize it as follows: that it used nationalism as did
all fascism, that it used racism, that it used symbols of
the nation (you know the controversy about the old
flag of the empire as against the new republican flag —
there were many such quarrels over symbols). It used
this kind of appeal to the past, but at the same time it
promised a future outside the problems of industrialization, outside the problems of urbanization, outside
the problems of revolution and counterrevolution,
outside the problems of inflation — in other words,
outside the problems of the day, including unemployment — all the problems which actually
existed. It said, by recapturing the past, we will determine a future which is a German future when every
German will get back his individual dignity and his
piece of land. To summarize it, when there will be a
hierachy of function but not of status. The Nazis did
not want to abolish political or economic hierarchy; on
the contrary, they were to be strengthened . But at the
same time a person's worth was said to exist independently of such hierarchies within which he functioned
in daily life, that his status depended upon his race and
his service to the national-socialist state. Here the most
menial occupation could coexist with a feeling of importance within the Nazi party or at national festivals.
The uniforms testified to a status which transcended
the daily function within economic or political reality.
This is, of course, common to all fascism, and its appeal
in times of crisis was enormous because fascism promised upward mobility, however spurious, to a much
greater extent than socialism could promise.

Ledeen: There are two things about this that puzzle me
a bit: the first is why you call this a looking forward.

Isn't this look forward really a look backward vaguely disguised? After all, the so-called New World that national socialism promised to create, the giving of a new kind of humanity to the Germans, really isn't a new world at all; it's the old. It's a vision of what the old used to be like before Germany was subjected to modernization and industrialization.

Mosse: That you see isn't quite true. Let us look for a minute at what the Nazis almost immediately did in the factory. Let us go to the base. Two things happened. First of all, (copied from Italy) there was the total organization of leisure time — a paternalism, if you like, but a paternalism which made the workers participate in cultural activities as they never had before. There were theater troupes, for example, in the factories. Secondly, and still more important, is what the Nazis called "beauty at work." Now I stress this because it has somehow been neglected. What the Nazis did by giving rebates in taxes (under the guidance of Albert Speer,[14] by the way) was to force factory owners to modernize. For the first time some of the German factory workers got decent working conditions, light and air, decent sanitation, decent washrooms. It was a kind of paternalism, if you like, but it wasn't against modernism. At the same time, as we know, the Nazis happily betrayed the small entrepreneur for the large economic units which were very modern and forward-looking. So you always have a combination. On the one hand, they appeal to the past, to the Aryan, to the German, to the peasant. On the other hand, modernization of factories, economic concentration. All of this is wrapped within an ideological cocoon which stresses nature, air and light, and antiindustrialism. Again, I come back to a dialectic, antiindustrialism and industrialism. in fascism are not so far removed from one another; they come together in political reality.

Ledeen: It's not at all surprising to find in the modern world a regime which says one thing and does something quite different. But what I had in mind when I asked you the question was a remark that DeFelice made in *Fascism: an Informal Introduction*[15] when he said that the new Nazi man, so to speak, was really the old Aryan, that ideal type that the Nazis strove toward was really something which had already existed. It wasn't as if progress were going to bring about the creation of a new human type—that human type was already there, it was the Aryan man. It was a question of liberating him from the encumbrances of the urban and the industrial worlds.

Mosse: Well, that is true for the vast majority of the Nazis. But in another sense for some Nazis, and we must talk here in different terms about Himmler and the SS[16], the new man did not exist — not just because he's oppressed but because he hasn't yet been bred. For many Nazis (not for Hitler) the ideal German was a figure from the past, let us say, Hermann or Arminius who beat the Roman legions. Somebody like that, with his blond looks and Aryan stereotype. The race is unchanged, that is why we must not make too much contact between racial thought and Darwinism — that's always done, totally mistaken quite often, because selection cannot improve the race. On the other hand, there is a trend of thought in national socialism, as I said, typified by Himmler and the SS, that indeed the new man has to be bred. This was never successfully institutionalized but attempted in what was called *lebensborn*.[17]

Let me make another rather important remark here. The new German man for others, including

Hitler, was not a man of the Teutonic forests, not Hermann the German. The new German man was the ideal bourgeois. That is to say, national socialism and racism annexed every middle-class virtue which was under siege in modern times — honest work, cleanliness, loyalty, a neat appearance. It said we will in fact reestablish these values in Germany by destroying the Jewish middle class which was thought to have corrupted them. Once you get rid of the Jewish middle class traditional values will be fine again. As a matter of fact, the new man of national socialism was the ideal bourgeois, and only in rhetoric did he have a connection with the ancient Aryan.

Ledeen: Can we say a few words about the ideal German woman in this context?

Mosse: The ideal German woman was the ideal woman of the nineteenth century. We must understand that for Hitler, Himmler, all of these people, their ideal time was the time of the German empire, what we call the Indian summer of the bourgeois world. So they accepted, for example, the middle class ideal of man and the romantic ideal of woman. Let us remember that in the eighteenth century women were already semiemancipated. It was largely the romantic movement during the nineteenth century which helped to put an end to the emancipation of women. Hitler undoubtedly believed that women belonged in the home. They were not allowed to study. There's a very typical film of 1936 called *Youth Goes to the Führer* in which the Hitler youth marched from all over Germany to Nuremberg. In that film no factories appear: Germany is a totally underdeveloped country, but women only appear once — for a folk dance. That is all. It's very typical.

Here we come into a conflict which is inherent in

Italian fascism, I think, as much as in national socialism. On the one hand you have an ideal of a male society, and on the other hand you have the necessity of upholding middle-class ideals. Let me define what I mean by middle-class ideals. There is no doubt that the turn from the eighteenth to the nineteenth century saw a great change in the moral tone of society; Harold Nicolson has characterized this change as the "onslaught of respectability." It meant that a new emphasis was put upon the gospel of work, sexual shame and restraint, moderation in everything, together with renewed stress upon the importance of the family. I call this middle-class morality because it was that class which at first carried it against the unbought grace of life of the aristocracy, though it soon became a generally accepted morality. Not only the middle class but workers and aristocracy became decent in the modern sense. The Nazis certainly claimed to protect such respectability symbolized by their clean cut young men who marched down the street. Indeed, everywhere the Right benefited from this ideal. We tend to forget how relatively recent it had become generally accepted.

But these ideals were bound to come into conflict with that activism which the Nazis needed in order to benefit by the disorder and near civil war which their storm troopers created before the Nazi seizure of power. This comes out very well in a document from the 1920s when a troop of SA discussed, What shall we do tonight? It was Christmas night, and the question was, Shall we go home to our families or beat up Communists? You see, the question was, Shall we uphold the bourgeois virtues for which we stand, or create disorder? Such activism caused as much trouble for Hitler as it did for Mussolini. Middle-class ideals and ideals of Greek beauty — a strong tradition in Germany — joined in creating the Aryan stereotype who owed nothing to the ancient Germanic past. However, ideals of nature — the importance of being close to Germanic nature — provided the setting for the ideal man and his connection with the ancient past. All of these ideas were bundled up and became transformed into the "beauty of work" in factories and into attempts — never successful by the way — to make garden cities and settlements. Hitler never cared for this, he thought it was quite phony. But there is variety here. And we must also make a distinction between the public and private. Public Nazi architecture we all know about, but much private architecture continued in the Weimar *Bauhaus* style.

Ledeen: How important was race in all of this? How central was the concept of race to national socialism?

Mosse: I obviously think it was very central indeed, as I have written that national socialism was an anti-Jewish revolution; a displaced revolution. It couldn't be an economic or social revolution, so it focused its revolution upon the Jews. I think that's very central, because you needed an antitype to the ideal. The idea of race needs an antitype and the Jew was it. The Jew never found a place in the liturgy, that is, all the things which meant uplift. The Jew had no role among the positive symbols such as the holy flame, the new man, and so forth. The Jew entered as a counterimage. This of course is mainly true in the German case.

Ledeen: Yes. It is clearly not true in many other countries, but we will come back to that later on when we discuss the question of fascism in general.

Mosse: Let me just add something here. The Jewish question was not *always* crucial. Racism itself could at times be pro-Jewish, and that is a very important point. The opinion of several respectable German racists at the end of the nineteenth century was that the Jews were Aryans. No question about it. And that was confirmed by the famous racial survey of Jews and Gentiles made by Rudolf Virchow at that time, which found so many blonde and blue-eyed Jews. So racism isn't always antisemitic, and I think again that while it is certainly inherent in all racism that the Jew is the victim, for the Jew represented the only foreign culture within Europe — different language, different dress, and different appearance for pious Jews — it was not a *necessary* development. German nationalism simply was not always antisemitic. But here again Jews had a certain visibility, especially in 1918 and 1919. They led revolutions, Kurt Eisner in Bavaria, Bela Kun in Hungary, you can go through the list, and above all in the Soviet Union — the Politburo had what some thought a disproportionate number of Jews — and so what used to be considered the Jewish capitalist conspiracy suddenly became transformed into the Jewish-Bolshevik-capitalist conspiracy, and you can trace this development after 1917.

Ledeen: You know, there was even a rumor at one point in Austria that D'Annunzio was the son of Palestinian Jews.

Mosse: Yes, you see for conspiracy ideals you must always have a foil, whether it's the Jews or the Americans or God knows what. Once you have a conspiracy you have to have a foil, and of course Hitler believed that all his enemies conspired together: the Jews, the Communists, the capitalists. Indeed there is a Nazi novel in which the young man is a Communist and the father is a banker and in the end the two of them worked together to destroy Germany.

Ledeen: I fully agree. Now, in your discussion of the

origins of national socialism you found that the two major traditional explanations were unsatisfactory. I am referring to the liberal explanation, which viewed national socialism as a sort of temporary explosion of irrationality — a country gone insane; and the traditional Marxist explanation of national socialism as a desperate attempt by industrial capitalism to defend itself against the threat of communism and social revolution. Could you explain why you found these models unsatisfactory?

Mosse: In the Marxist literature of the 1930s and 1940s there were several analyses. One analysis was, as you said, that national socialism was the last defense of capitalism. And another analysis went back to Marx himself where in *The Eighteenth Brumaire of Louis-Napoleon Bonaparte* Marx points out the authoritarian potential of liberalism. And he does that in a discussion of Bonapartism. So many Marxist historians in the '30s and '40s saw national socialism not only as a defense of capitalism — as the last stage of capitalism — but also as a consequence of liberalism, which had within it this Bonapartist element as Marx had thought way back in 1870. It was particularly Herbert Marcuse who mined this vein of historical interpretation. And yet I think we must say that the research since then has conclusively demonstrated that while big business supported national socialism to a certain degree, it never did so wholeheartedly or indeed provided the major money for the party.

Ledeen: Where did most of the money come from?

Mosse: The money came from individual contributions. All this is not a secret now that we have the documents, and I think that historical theories must fit the documents. The old canard about big business and the Third Reich must be modified. Now there are two modern theories . . .

Ledeen: Just a minute. Before we get to the modern Marxist theories, could you tell us what was the extent of the support big business gave to the Nazis?

Mosse: I can't give you the exact figure, but it was not very substantial before 1933. Big business had its own parties which it supported — above all the German National Party — but I think the important point here is the theory of Tim Mason[18] which explains that the success of national socialism was due in part to its lack of economic commitment. It nationalized when it wanted to nationalize, like the Hermann Goering works, which were major steel nationalizations. It allied itself with big business when it wanted such an alliance, but what Tim Mason calls "the primacy of politics" always prevailed. It is quite true that none of the Nazis had an economic theory as such. Economics was always subordinated to their political and racial aims.

Now the third major Marxist theory comes from a German scholar, Reinhard Kühnl,[19] who believes that fascism is not a creature of monopoly capitalism, but that indeed fascism was a movement which stood on its own two feet, and which really provided the mass base for the defense of capitalism. This isn't the simple formula that national socialism was the creature of capitalism, but rather it states that national socialism was its own movement with its own criteria which are not directly connected to capitalism or to capitalist desires.

Ledeen: Even though it serves the function of defending capitalism?

Mosse: Eventually it brings a mass base to the defense of capitalism. Now the problem with Kühnl's theory is fairly simple: it makes fascism out to be something really unique and something that again is caught and manipulated by monopoly capitalism. But there is not the slightest documentary evidence that Krupp or Thyssen[20] manipulated Hitler. The evidence is all the other way, so none of these theories are taken very seriously any more. Among Marxist historians themselves there is a trend away from such oversimplifications.[21] I should say that when these theories came up in the '30s and '40s we didn't have all the documentation that we have today. Indeed, some of these theories about the relationship of national socialism to monopoly capitalism are pure theory, and are not based on any hard evidence whatsoever. They are not connected to any troublesome facts.

Now, the theory that national socialism comes out of liberalism or is some inevitable consequence of liberalism — a theory that goes back to Marx, who pronounced it under quite different circumstances in 1870 — is also a highly questionable one. Again, it goes in for the conspiracy theory: the liberal bourgeoisie unable to keep its status now conspires with a racist movement which will give it back its status. I would put it this way: we must distinguish between liberalism as a political movement and liberalism as a set of values. Liberalism as a set of so-called middle-class values quite clearly was adopted by national socialism and aided the movement, as I have said before. Liberalism as a political movement was quite ineffective after 1918, but inasmuch as it was effective, it fought national socialism. It made no peace with national socialism to the degree that many other movements did. In other words, I think we must say that liberalism as a political movement behaved better than, let us say,

some of the Conservative party or even some of the
Communist party who went in for joint strikes with
Nazis, like the Berlin transport workers' strike.

To put it another way, all these movements — communism, liberalism, conservatism, socialism — were
trapped by the fact that national socialism determined
the terrain of debate. That is why you have the famous
appeal by the Communist leader Hans Neumann to
the Nazis against a fratricidal war,[22] and the adoption
by the Communist party in the last years of nationalism
of antisemitic stances (which they'd already done once
before in 1923 with Radek's speech glorifying Schlage-
ter, the Nazi martyr who fought against French occupation). To put it simply, all of these movements were
to a certain extent caught in the tide of nationalism and
responded to it partly by trying to co-opt it. There is
nothing special here about liberalism, nothing whatsoever. Indeed, I think it would be true to say that
liberalism continued in the Third Reich through
Jewish organizations which were always the most liberal. The last voice of liberalism, tolerance, and
pluralism in Germany is to be found in Jewish newspapers and writings in the Third Reich. You can find
this in virtually all the Jewish publications, even among
the Zionist ones. But these were in any case a minority.

To blame liberalism for the success of the Nazis is,
therefore, a kind of theory of monopoly capitalism
sneaking in through the back door. And it isn't at all
convincing.

Ledeen: What about the liberal explanation of the success of national socialism? I am referring to the view
that Nazism represents a kind of temporary madness,
an interruption of the normal flow of events.

Mosse: There are really two liberal models. One is, as
you say, the theory of a pure aberration, but that isn't

really worth discussing. More relevant is Professor Ernst Nolte's theory[23] that the bourgeoisie as it were reached out to national socialism in a crisis and that when the crisis was over they again became good bourgeois. There is, of course, something to it, but I think that it omits the element of mass politics and political leadership. In other words, I return again to what I said earlier: it omits elements in national socialism which were a general response to a crisis, which is not unique perhaps to this particular crisis, but is an ongoing response.

More serious, I think, than this is the liberal idea which judges everything from the perspective of parliamentary government, which thinks that parliamentary government is the only possible model for democracy. That is also a blinder as far as historical interpretations are concerned, for it is just not true. In the first place, European parliamentary governments have never withstood severe crises. In the 1920s the German parliament, the Italian parliament, and the Portugese parliament all committed suicide. We can say that parliamentary government is only something for quiet times, but it has never been anything else. Therefore, these liberals who are wedded to a parliamentary regime and its nature overlook the fact that for millions participation in politics is not participation through voting every couple of years but through mass rallies, mass marches, myth, and symbolism. The liberals play this down, and they believe somehow that every movement in our time must be viewed in terms of parliamentary government — a parliamentary government which has never withstood crises very well in Europe.[24]

Chapter Three

Ledeen: Now one might want to say that the bulk of your work on national socialism has represented an attempt to deal with the creation of a national socialist consensus. You have always insisted that national socialism represented the tastes and desires of many Germans. In fact, in *The Nationalization of the Masses* you put it this way: "the accusation that through propaganda the Nazis attempted to erect a terrorist world of illusions can be upheld only in part. Enough evidence has accumulated to account for the genuine popularity of Nazi literature and art which did not need the stimulus of terrorism to become effective. This is true for the Nazi political style as well. It was popular because it was built on a familiar and genial tradition."[25] Are you arguing that national socialism is part of a long political tradition?

Mosse: Yes, of course, national socialism fastened onto several traditions — the tradition of nationalism, the tradition of mass movement, and the shorter tradition of middle-class morality. It promised at first both activism and law and order. For a Germany rent by civil war and economic crisis this was no simple matter. I would go further and say that as Hitler managed through public works to rid Germany of six million unemployed within a year, there is always the objective reality which gave credibility to Hitler's rhetoric. It was extremely difficult for most Germans to resist this kind of temptation. I know people who voted for the Nazis just because they liked the clean-cut young men walking through the streets. National socialism stood for good old values. This is I think quite clear.

Ledeen: Well, this will seem paradoxical to a lot of people who identify national socialism with the violence of the Nazis — the concentration camps, the war, the genocide, and so forth.

Mosse: The concentration camp system didn't really start until 1936. In 1934 there were only a few camps and people came and went after waves of arrests. It's not really until 1937 that you get the concentration camp system established though the early individual camps were brutal enough. But in 1937 permanent internment became official policy because of the need for forced labor under the four-year plan. At the beginning all that the Nazis proclaimed was the exclusion of the Jews from public life. Nobody except Hitler thought of murdering anybody. Even if you didn't agree with the antisemitism, the positive might easily have outweighed the negative. For where were you going to turn? You may have had a class-conscious proletariat, but it is still true that the Left parties, like the Center parties, vanished like the driven snow and that while terror existed it was not too obtrusive at the start. I think it is generally agreed that part of Hitler's tactic was that if you didn't resist in the first two years then it became ever more difficult, then there was ever more obtrusive terror, then it meant being a martyr. As there was a general enthusiasm in the first two years

and as Hitler seemed moderate, when there was a call
for resistance it was too late. You had to resist early or
else you were in danger of life and limb.

Ledeen: I want to postpone for one minute the discussion of the development of the Nazi regime — of the
form that it took subsequently — to finish with the
discussion of the origins of national socialism and its
historical context. With all of your discussion of the
necessity of putting national socialism in a long historical context, of discussing it in terms of a development
from the wars of liberation against Napoleon to the
national socialist *Machtergreifung,* you still insist on the
centrality of World War I. The question is, how do you
reconcile the centrality of the war with your insistence
on this very long overview?

Mosse: As I have said before, you need a tradition, but
it's World War I that activated that tradition. It's
World War I that created Hitler, who was, after all, a
kind of war hero, a soldier — he was blinded in the war
as you may remember. The Nazis made much of the
war spirit. So you must say that in Germany this became very important. In England and France it wasn't
that important at all. In England, for example, one
general wrote his memoirs, "Why I Became a Murderer." But in Germany this would have been impossible. The spirit of the war also meant a kind of bridge
over defeat and revolution, counterrevolution, and
inflation. Perhaps I can illustrate this best by citing the
introduction to a book which describes most, I think,
seven hundred monuments to the war dead in Germany — a book put out by the republic — which says
that the fallen in World War I haven't died at all. They
come back to every German in his dreams and exhort

him to perform a German miracle, that is, revenge for the defeat. The war had created a race of heroes, if you like. So it was always said — during the Nazi period, for example, when Hitler annexed Austria — that he placed his victory on the tomb of the fallen soldiers. This vocabulary was always present.

Ledeen: Do you think the war created any new values? Did the war provide anything that wasn't there in the traditions to start with or was it just a catalyst?

Mosse: The only new thing the war provided all over Europe was a brutalization of life. That brutalization of life came with the glorification of mass death on a scale never seen before. It came with the massacres that took place during the war. Let us remember that in 1915 and 1916 the Turks massacred seven hundred thousand Armenians. All of this led to a kind of glorification of brutality under the guise of struggle which in Germany carried over into the post-war world. What happened after 1918 in Germany was not only what I've talked about so much, revolution and counterrevolution, but also a kind of civil war waged by the Right, including political murders like the murder of Walter Rathenau[26], the foreign minister, in 1922 and many others. So that indeed this brutalization from the war carried over into the postwar period, I think in Italy as well. It is on that, in a sense, that fascism fed as well — taking brutalization up as a kind of activism and then combining it not only with the worship of heroes and the worship of the fallen but also with middle-class morality and law and order and all of that.

Ledeen: That is, it takes the violence of the war as a

virtue and then uses the fear of the violence that the war has produced as a method of organizing the middle class.

Mosse: No, as a matter of perpetuating the values of the middle class. I would say that before 1914 there was Nietzsche, who glorified struggle in and of itself. But Nietzsche was a poet. After 1918 Mussolini, Hitler, and other similar leaders began to glorify struggle as a way of life. The war hasn't ended, we continue the war. Some historians said that this spirit existed after the wars of liberation, but never with such consistency or density. It is what I call the brutalization of life which comes after World War I and which I think is still with us to a very great extent.

Ledeen: Do you get any kind of elitism after World War I? Do you get any kind of notion of the creation of the natural elite — men who had proved their courage and their virtues in the trenches of World War I and that should be transferred perhaps into the political scene of Germany after the war?

Mosse: Well, of course the idea of the storm troopers is very important because of the kind of war it was. It was trench warfare, and this new kind of warfare had created an elite which had gone over the top. This was made into myth in Germany above all by Ernst Jünger in his *Storm of Steel* (1922) and in his war diaries. There were also those who talked of a new race of men who knew no fear such as Oswald Spengler whose *Decline of the West* (which was written during the war let us remember) ends with a race of barbarians. There was a great deal of this glorifying of primitive force, and in Germany it became reality through the so-called Free

Corps — the soldiers who refused to demobilize and who independently continued to fight the Poles in the east and then, of course, the French during the Ruhr occupation. They fought real battles in the east, from which emerged the myth (important for the future) of the Free Corps which had saved upper Silesia for Germany (which, by the way, is true) — men and officers, a new race of men who were wrongly thought to be totally unideological in the sense that they called themselves "fighters without a flag." The government didn't support them because the republic could not really condone this. Yet they fought for the nation. So you have these Free Corps and their leaders who were also involved in many of the political murders. These leaders very often became Nazis. Himmler was in that circle and so was Höss, the commandant of Auschwitz, who was sentenced to several years in prison for a political murder. So quite a few people, especially in the concentration camp world, came from this kind of background.

Ledeen: What about the structure within the Free Corps? Is it a hierarchical structure?

Mosse: It was the kind of thing which Europeans had dreamt about since the 1880s — it was supposed to be a community of affinity not a community of force. The same sort of ideal which the German youth movement symbolized — a banding together of people linked by affinity who elect a leader as the first among equals and who becomes the leader because he does things better — he shoots better, he marches better, he has more iron will. You have that in the German youth movement and in these chiefs of the Free Corps: Escherich, Erhardt[27]. They were a sort of condottieri—

not on a commercial basis, but on the basis of a search for a true national community.

Ledeen: What's the relationship between this and the Führer principle, if any?

Mosse: Well, that *is* the Führer principle in fact — the modern Führer principle which had already been summarized earlier by Gustav LeBon[28] in France. Mussolini knew of LeBon and Hitler copied a great deal of *Mein Kampf* from LeBon's book, *The Crowd* (1895). Above all, Hitler took the notion that the leader must be part of the crowd, that he must share the myths everyone else shares, but share them to a greater and stronger extent. The leader arises from the masses. There was, in fact, a national socialist ceremony where Hitler marched as part of the masses and only in the end emerged to deliver his speech. This was supposed to be a leadership determined by function, by being part of the new race of heroes.

Ledeen: This brings us to one of the central topics in any discussion of national socialism, which is the discussion of Hitler — Hitler himself, Hitler's role, Hitler's theories. Let's talk about what may seem to be a very banal question in some respects: what is the relationship between *Mein Kampf* and the practice of national socialism?

Mosse: Well, it is very close in a way, although *Mein Kampf* was written when Hitler was in prison after his coup of 1923 to enable him to make a comeback. He thought he must have a self-glorifying autobiography and theoretical statement. In reality, of course, there is a great deal of truth in *Mein Kampf*, although we know that some things aren't true. Hitler writes that he came to Vienna as a poor boy; he didn't. But misleading statements in *Mein Kampf* are, I would say, minor. *Mein Kampf* is devoted 50 percent to theory and 50 percent to organization. And that's about right as far as Hitler is concerned because he believed that theory was all important — the myth was central — but it would be no good unless it could be translated into action. And that's what *Mein Kampf* is all about.

Ledeen: So that *Mein Kampf* was really a kind of primer for national socialism, a guide for national socialists.

Mosse: It may have become so. The national socialist movement was never oriented towards the written word — always towards liturgy and symbol — so that I wonder how many people actually read *Mein Kampf*. Everybody had it. But if you read *Mein Kampf* then I think there are several things in there which are convincing. What Hitler says about organization or also how he became an anti-Semite, for example. Hitler believed what he wrote about the Jews in *Mein Kampf*.

Ledeen: You believe the story about his coming to Vienna and seeing the East European pious Jews and so forth?

Mosse: Very much. Because I believe antisemitism in Europe was a clash of cultures. There is much evidence (Hitler is not the only one) that if you had lived surrounded by the assimilated Jews in Linz where he was brought up and you came to Vienna and saw the nonassimilated Jews who were coming in from Galicia, that a provincial boy might get a fright. A lot of people did. And if, in addition, you have a turn of mind which is already attuned to the mysterious, the occult, and at the same time you're in touch with the sort of racist

sects which proliferated in Vienna and, which believed
in the occult in a kind of racist theosophy, then it all
comes together.

There is now a school of historians[29] which says that
Hitler was never really antisemitic in Vienna. I cannot
possibly accept that. I think the evidence for that is
very feeble. These are psycho-historians who believe
the crucial fact in Hitler's development of hatred toward the Jews was not Vienna, but that his mother died
in the care of a Jewish doctor. They emphasize his
blinding at the end of the war, his stay in hospital, his
hallucinations, and they say, in essence, that he suddenly woke up and hated the Jews. I don't believe that
at all. I think this experience perhaps strengthened
him in his hatred. Until 1918 his antisemitism may
have been vague and occult, but after 1918 he came
into contact with Dietrich Eckardt[30] who became his
political mentor and who believed in the Jewish
Bolshevik-capitalist conspiracy. Interestingly enough
Eckhardt did not want to murder the Jews, he wanted
to put them back into ghettos. The final solution represents, I think, Hitler's own ideas pushed to their
logical consequence. The people he was surrounded
with (including Himmler) did not think of a final solution.

Ledeen: Let's leave the final solution for just a second
because we'll get to that in the discussion of the evolution of national socialism.

Mosse: I should perhaps say something else. Hitler was
not only obsessed by race, but also by *lebensraum*:[31]
living space. From the beginning, race and living space
come together. The extermination of the Jews and the
expansion of Germany were all tied up in his brain,
certainly after 1923. By the 1930s at the latest he
seemed to have believed that you had to have expansion in order to exterminate the Jews. I want to make

that clear. There is no doubt whatsoever in my mind that, no matter how much Hitler disguised it, the anti-Jewish revolution was his revolution. Drumont in France thought the same way: if you somehow got rid of the Jews and distributed their money and their wealth it would make an enormous difference, it would make possible a greater equality. If you got rid of the Jews you could restore and secure middle-class morality. Hitler simply took these ideas and infused them with a goodly dose of occultism, because he also believed in secret sciences — vital ethers which come from another world — and that the Aryan was born in a burst of lightning. So he infused this with the kind of crazy, racial sectarianism he had learned in Vienna.

Ledeen: So one really finds some exceedingly contradictory elements in Hitler doesn't one? On the one hand, you said that as a good bourgeois he wants to uphold solid middle-class values—he's an apostle of law and order, he believes in a solid home, the tradition of the bourgeois family, a normal life. Yet at the same time he holds a whole series of nutty ideas about the origin of this bourgeois world—he thinks it all rests on an otherworldly base, that it comes from supernatural forces and a mystical realm of reality. How do you reconcile these elements?

Mosse: Well, it isn't easy to reconcile, but it's easy to see. He was not the only one who fused the racial idea with the spiritualism so popular at the turn of the century. Quite a few did that. These were, after all, two important trends at the end of the century. Nationalism was also common, along with the idea of living space. What is extraordinary and in the end fatal, was that these elements — along with the traditional, bourgeois ones we've talked about — came together in a man who became what we call in Germany (and there were many other like him) a wandering prophet, what Hitler himself called somewhat disparagingly in *Mein Kampf* a volkish[32] prophet. But Hitler also believed that these ideas had to be actualized, and it so happened that he had a political genius in two things: he learned his lessons—after he had failed in the putsch of 1923 he saw that he would have to come to power legally—and he had an absolutely superb sense of political timing. So everything, you see, came together in Hitler. Why? I have no idea.

Ledeen: Alright. Now in the development of the national socialist party Hitler is of course the central figure—he's the crucial moment, he's the one who gives the national socialist party a sense of political direction, isn't he? Prior to Hitler there had been a group of people with these same strange ideas.

Mosse: Not a group of people, a group of workers—a group of railroad workers. There is, you see, an unsolved problem as a matter of fact. In Germany as in France the nucleus of these rightist movements were railroad workers. I have no explanation for that, but it is true.

Ledeen: What is the role of workers in general in the national socialist party?

Mosse: In Germany in general they are at the fringe, but at the frontier of Germany they are very strong. For example, the German speaking workers of Bohemia and Moravia who first formed a kind of national socialist movement quite separate from Hitler became national socialists because of pressure from the Czechs—the competition of the Czechs. In a sense this beginning of what we might call national socialism in Germany (if you call Bohemia or Moravia Germany regions, and they were German speaking regions) was a workers' movement, and it is that workers' movement which shaded off into the first German national socialist workers party. But you see Hitler's genius was to lift this movement from a little sectarian workers' movement which it might have remained, into a middle-class movement. After all, we have the statistics—by 1930 roughly 25 percent of the party were workers, which is small, but not as inconsiderable as is sometimes made out.

Ledeen: Do you mean party members or party voters?

Mosse: Party members. You can have a working-class fascism in some countries—in Rumania and in Hungary where we know that the Arrow Cross[33] was largely made up of industrial workers—but here I believe in the theory of Juan Linz that in countries where there was a strong socialist movement you couldn't have a working-class fascism. You could have it only in countries like Rumania[34] and Hungary where socialist movements were suppressed; there fascism provided the instrument to mobilize the masses. This was not true in Germany. So we mustn't exaggerate what I have said. The party in a sense got some of its inspirations from these frontier workers' movements. But Hitler then immediately lifted it to a middle-class party.

Ledeen: And in the creation of this middle-class party you see a central role in Hitler's organization of national socialist festivals. What is the role of the liturgy and the ritual in the success of national socialism?

Mosse: Liturgy and ritual would not have succeeded without organization at the base. But liturgy and ritual were very important for several reasons. First, they gave the movement a dynamism where other parties had bureaucracies and you had to be quite old before you could succeed. The Nazi party was a party of

youth. Hitler was young, they were all young. Liturgy
and festival typified this dynamism, this mass participation which other parties had difficulty with—above
all the parties which were too didactic. The national
socialists quite rightly told their local party people
never to speak longer than fifteen minutes. In other
words, the speeches weren't important—they were always part of ritual. This is true for Hitler's speeches
too—the rhythm was important, not so much the content.

Ledeen: At this point it might be well to say something
about the German youth movement[35] and the extent
to which national socialism carries on a tradition of
youth movements.

Mosse: All fascisms were youth movements—in a sense
that has very little to do with the specific German
movement. You can go through the ages of the leaders. The German youth movement is something else
again, and it opposed national socialism to a large
degree. It was a search for community—youth among
itself. It started out in 1901 with roaming in the countryside, getting inspiration for what they called a true
nationalism from the Germanic landscape rather than
from saber rattling. It was the first movement where
boys between the ages of fourteen and eighteen years
could hike without adult supervision. After the war it
became evermore politicized. There were leftwing
youth movements, but they were usually tied to political parties. But the youth movements that we might say
were more on the Right—nationalists—were not tied
to political parties, at least not formally. They tended
to be sympathetic to a great variety of rightist parties,
including the German national party. But not to national socialism, which they thought was too crude (this
was middle-class youth, remember)—too controlled by
adults. The Nazi youth movement was controlled by

the party and therefore was not a true community. In the end, the Nazis smashed the German youth movement like they smashed everything else. But some of the Nazi attitudes were also found in the German youth movements—some of them carried on, to a certain extent, racism and nationalism in their communities.

Ledeen: Is there an element of generational conflict explicitly in national socialism where Hitler claims to represent the young forces of Germany—the young Germans against the old Germans, the new Germany against the old Germany?

Mosse: No, Hitler put it a little differently, and of course again it was a brilliant tactic—he claimed to represent the young Germany against the bourgeoisie and thereby connected with many protest movements of the end of the nineteenth century where youth rebelled against their elders. Such movements were also, remember, always a protest against liberalism. In the literature of the 1880s, '90s, and the early 1900s the revolt of youth against their elders is a revolt against positivism, Darwinism, capitalism, and liberalism. Hitler tried to carry this on, to adopt their rhetoric. He was against the bourgeois. What he meant by that was that he was against the elders. What elders? The elders in the other political parties—the bureaucrats, the parliamentarians, who were far from heroic. I remember D'Annunzio's description of the Italian parliament, "shifty-looking people with pot bellies." Well Hitler did the same. He took the part of youth and extolled the vitality of youth. That's very attractive because remember—at least I can speak for America—even in our student riots of the 1960s, many middle-aged professors who understood nothing of Herbert Marcuse, were on the side of youth simply because they liked youth. Hitler fully annexed that revolt, but in reality it was again a tactic. It was a revolt of youth against the bourgeois in the name of the bourgeois. In a sense that statement is also true of the German youth movements.[36]

Ledeen: So it's a peculiar phenomenon: Hitler leads an anti-bourgeois revolution of the bourgeois.

Mosse: Yes, except there is always within it the problem of activism and civil war. Fascism had to create civil war to come to power anywhere. And thus followed the activism—the SA in the streets singing that "Jewish blood springs from the knife", beating up communists in the evening. But in the end the bill had to be paid, and in 1934 Hitler did away with the SA. Mussolini had a similar problem.

Ledeen: Why did Hitler do away with them?

Mosse: Because now he had to have his law and order bourgeois morality and it could not really be reconciled with these toughs. Anyhow the SA was in danger of becoming too powerful, so he killed both birds with one stone: he assassinated their leaders and brought the organization under control. The immediate cause was the army, since if he wanted to have the support of the army he had to get rid of these toughs who were a rival army. But all these elements play into it. I think Mussolini had to make a similar choice, they both had to choose in their moment of truth. Before they got to power they could do a balancing act between activism and middle-class respectability, but then in all fascism there comes the moment where it has to choose middle-class respectability and somehow cope with the toughs. There were exceptions when an unchecked activism took over, and then even the Nazis were horrified. When the Iron Guard in Romania briefly came to power, the toughs took over. There were massacres.

There was disorder. And the Nazis promptly helped destroy the Iron Guard. Their leaders went into exile in Germany.

Ledeen: How would you characterize Hitler personally? There's been a lot of literature recently which portrays Hitler as a real psychotic, as a sexual deviant, as a pervert.

Mosse: There's nothing to that. No documents, nothing supports that. Rather the documents support the fact that Hitler was normal within his mysticism, which we discussed. But there were lots of other people who believed in such occult ideas. Hitler's sex life was a normal sex life. We know enough about that to be quite sure. Eva Braun was a little country girl who deeply loved Hitler. He deeply loved her. If he treated her badly it was because he believed, perhaps quite rightly, that a leader cannot be a father of a family, that he must have this activist, new-race-of-men image. And a little country girl really didn't belong. There is nothing to the theory that Hitler was a deviant. It is a very facile explanation because if Hitler were a psychopath why don't we study psychoanalysis instead of politics? Some American has now suggested after Nixon that all political leaders see a psychoanalyst. I am not sure this would improve matters. But still Hitler was normal. He was also charming at some times and very modest at others. He had a kind of shyness about him. In other words, in no way did he give the impression of being a monster. People who met him in one situation thought very highly of him, in another situation he was quite different. That was perhaps his talent. If he came in contact with statesmen of other countries he was respectable and charming, but when he was among friends or associates and let himself go he was different. But I don't think he ever let himself go to any great extent. Here I really think the evidence of Albert Speer is the evidence most to be relied upon.

Ledeen: We've spoken about Hitler's personality, about the centrality of Hitler in the national socialist experience. A great deal of your understanding about Hitler came from your conversations and your reading of Albert Speer.

Mosse: I think Speer was extremely helpful in my understanding of Hitler, yes, but I had already gotten some understanding from other sources as well.

Ledeen: Did you get anything new from Speer that you hadn't had before?

Mosse: Of course. Speer's memoirs are, in my opinion, the single best portrait of Hitler as he was in private life. Speer tells what it was like to live at the court of Adolf Hitler, and he stresses some points of very great importance—that Hitler looked back as the ideal period to the fin de siecle period in Austria or to Wilhelminian Germany as I've said before, and not to any mythical Germanic past. He was provincial in his outlook, in his tastes, and the only thing which made him so fatal to mankind was his racism. But when his racism or his political judgment didn't come through, he was indeed banal. He loved the neo-classicism of Vienna—that to him was great German art. The Vienna Opera was always the most beautiful building for him. The great Vienna street, the Ringstrasse, sent him into ecstacy—these are the tastes of the generation of founders, the bourgeois taste of the end of the century. Similarly, as I have said, his ideas of manners and morals all came from that period. There is a passage in Speer's memoirs where Hitler said that the rifles which were good enough for him in World War I were certainly good enough for the soldiers in World

War II. The Nazi arbiter of German painting, Gerdy Troost, the widow of his first architect, has written in retrospect that his taste in painting stopped in 1918. His whole outlook on the world stopped in 1918. But what gave him his dynamic? Race. That didn't stop in 1918. It went on, the kind of Manichean world of race and occultism which we've talked about.

Now Speer was the organizer of the festivals, of the political liturgy of the Third Reich. So what he told me about that, of course, was indispensable. I'll give you two examples. One is the influence of the modern dance of the 1920s that you cannot find in any book[37]—the other the possible influence of modern jazz and its rhythm on these liturgies. I got this from these conversations, so that indeed there are still many important insights which we must get from interviews with people who played a leading part in these events. Not everything is written down. As far as the survivors of the regime are concerned, Speer is undoubtedly the most important because he was in many ways the closest to Hitler, and is also I think today the most honest witness.

Ledeen: Do you think that basically we are in possession of sufficient information and data about national socialism so that our judgments about it can be taken with relative confidence, or do you think that we are still only at the first stage of approximation?

Mosse: I think my answer is best put by Renzo DeFelice in his introduction to his *Mussolini and Hitler*[38] where he says in effect that there may be new documents which will come to light but that they probably will not change anything fundamental in our interpretation or in our knowledge.

Chapter Four

Ledeen: Would you say that the evolution of national socialism under Hitler is simil~r to the evolution of fascism under Mussolini in the sense that it represents a rejection of some of the original premises and some of the original elements of the movement itself?

Mosse: No, I would not say so at all. The rhetoric of the SA that Jewish blood drips from the knife and the sporadic violence were rejected. Instead Hitler represented himself as a law and order moderate which he thought was important for a while. There are many examples: the Nazi program called only for the exclusion of the Jews from German life, and even that was done extremely slowly. Hitler always wanted to seem the pushed rather than the pusher. Before every anti-semitic legislation there were encouraged, to be sure, antisemitic riots. But you can't produce a riot from nothing, so there was certainly that feeling. You always have such disturbances before every measure, whether it is the boycott of Jewish shops or the exclusion of Jewish judges and lawyers. But when we come to the much misunderstood Nuremberg laws, of the four proposed versions Hitler chose the most moderate one. All that the Nuremberg laws said was that Jews could not marry Aryans and could not have Aryan servants. Nothing else. Hitler immediately said this is my final word on the Jewish question. As a result, in 1935 Jews began to return to Germany because you could certainly live with such a law. The point that I want to make very strongly is that Hitler's internal tactics were the same as his tactics on foreign policy: self-produced pressure, then action, and then the assertion that this is my final word. So everybody was confused until the time came to strike again.

Now I think this is quite different from Mussolini because Hitler from the beginning had a much more definite goal in mind. You could see from 1933 on (and even before) what Hitler wanted. I doubt whether you could ever really say in detail what sort of Italy Mussolini wanted, though I'm not sure.

Ledeen: As national socialism takes form, as the regime becomes more and more oppressive, as the concentration camps are built, is this part of an inner logic to national socialism or is it a response to certain unexpected developments?

Mosse: It's an inner logic of Hitler's goals. It's not necessarily an inner logic of the national socialist program. It is, however, an inner logic of racism, if you want to carry racism to its logical conclusion. The winter of 1937 is the vital date when everything changes—when Hitler first begins to tighten Jewish policy. Now you have to understand that until then for many the regime had proved to be surprisingly moderate. Jews could still live in Germany economically because it really wasn't until late 1937 that the Aryanization of most business begins. Even a Christian who converted to Judaism in 1937 could still get government grants, indigent Jews got unemployment compensation, and books could still be bought which were forbidden. So that until fairly late in 1937, however awful the regime was (and I don't want to say anything else but that it was awful), it was still livable for many people. There was only sporadic terror even against the Jews. There was separation; there was apartheid. Look how many people live in apartheid today. And it wasn't even apartheid in the South African sense in that the Jews were not yet properly separated out, so that everybody could say, "oh, look how reasonable it is." In foreign policy, one success after another; in internal economic policy one success after another. People didn't realize that these successes followed a kind of internal logic of rearmament, war and destruction. So in 1937—and I'm not saying anything that modern scholarship on the subject doesn't say—Hitler had preserved his image of moderation, of middle-class virtue, of law and order, and of no violence—no violence *ever* because after all the final solution wasn't individualized. What Hitler understood, you see, though he was a bad administrator, was how important the modern state and the modern bureaucracy were for his aims: you cannot have genocide without the modern state because to have genocide you have to catch *everybody,* and that you can only do, not through pogroms, but through bureaucracy, through the card file. Hitler realized something people have absolutely forgotten—that the extermination of a whole people is only possible in a modern state and not in an underdeveloped state.

Ledeen: Since you've said that for genocide you need a modern state and a modern bureaucracy, this brings us automatically, it seems to me, to the theory of Hannah Arendt. In her book *Eichmann in Jerusalem*[39] she introduces a very controversial thesis which really takes two forms, and I'd like to have you comment on both parts of the thesis. First she states that the destruction of the European Jews was carried out not by monsters but by integral components of the modern bureaucracy doing their jobs and following orders. The second part of the theory is that the Jews participated in this world and cooperated in the process itself.

Mosse: To comment on the first: I think with some qualification I quite agree. But one factor must be added to that of bureaucracy and duty: those people who actively participated in the final solution, and whose feelings we shall never know, were victims or products of the corrosion and corruption of middle-class values through national socialism. What I mean by this is that for them the Jews were the enemy who disturbed or destroyed these values. To keep these values intact the Jews had to be destroyed—this was doing their duty. I can illustrate it concretely by a rather famous passage from the memoirs of Rudolf Höss, the commandant of Auschwitz and the greatest mass murderer of all time, who wrote that while he was watching Jews going to their death in the gas chambers he was thinking about his home life, his dog, the flowering apple trees. In other words, there was a complete divorce from humanity of the people he was killing. Moreover, Höss goes further still and says these people behaved quite differently than I behaved in prison. When I was in prison we were upright and so on—but Jews behave like Jews. They fight over every bit of food, they betray each other, they claw each other. They are hardly human. And of course, again, this was a self-induced prophecy. He kept the Jews in Auschwitz on short rations so that they had to fight for food. The remarkable thing of course is that many Jews survived intact and that after the holocaust they could successfully organize the flight and rescue from

Europe to Palestine. Höss thought in terms of
stereotypes which he saw come true by a kind of self-
fulfilling prophecy. I would also say that the corruption of values for which these people stand is not
abnormal in our civilization. It's a part of a growing
brutalization—a part of the idea of total war which you
already have in World War I: the enemy must be
killed, and to kill the enemy is a good act. The church
blesses it, in fact.

There are several factors that must not be forgotten.
Not only was there an attempt to strip humanity from
the Jews, but the Jews went to their deaths nude, which
is very important. First of all, it robbed the Jews of all
defenses because they were middle-class people, something Hannah Arendt always forgot. It also makes
people look alike. So to Höss Jews looked like an undif-
ferentiated mass. There is a famous story in which
Himmler once pulled out a blond boy from a queue to
the gas chamber and asked him whether his parents
were really Jewish. The boy said they were, to which
Himmler replied that he was sorry to be unable to help
him. In other words the stereotype we talked about
was always involved. So I think this isn't the banality of
evil as Hannah Arendt calls it. It's difficult to think of
another title, but it is in a way an evil threatening the
twentieth century pushed to its extreme. I think there
is nothing banal about it. I don't think people like Höss
thought of it as banal. They thought—as in Himmler's
famous speech—we've seen all these corpses and we
still remain strong. They also thought of it as an extreme situation. So I think Hannah Arendt was not
right in calling it the banality of evil, but certainly she
was quite right in pointing out that these SS were not
what are commonly called monsters. With one part of
their being they were good neighbors, good wives,
good husbands.

Ledeen: We said before that Hitler represented the tastes and desires of Germans in most of the things he did. Did he represent the tastes and desires of the German public in the final solution?

Mosse: No. It was not even the tastes and desires of many SS. We know how astonished even Himmler was when the order for the final solution was given, first in secret and then in writing. In 1937 the Jewish Germans passed from the rather more gentle custody of the Ministry of Justice and Interior to the total custody of the SS. But only in 1937. The SS did give some thought of course to where the hundred of thousands of newly annexed Austrian Jews and the millions of Polish Jews could go. Who was to take them? Nobody wanted them. So in a sense you may say here the final solution was programmed. What the German people heard we shall never know. That is a very unprofitable speculation, because it is pure conjecture.

Ledeen: What about the Jews in all of this process?

Mosse: The Jews were middle class like the Germans, even more so. When a middle-class Jew or a high middle-class Jew (who was usually a leader of the Jews) sat opposite Eichmann, there was an evil that he couldn't fathom. Jews were liberals. They believed in the Enlightenment, and had no idea of the evil that awaited them. I think neither did many other people. This was the twentieth century after all—the enlightened century. The final solution was totally unthinkable. And if people heard about it, at first they put it on a level with the horror stories of World War I. Remember it was said that in World War I the Germans had cut off the hands of nurse Cavelle . . . all untrue. So if they heard something about this they may have thought it was just another horror story. That was the only precedent to go by. So I do not think you can fault the Jews. I mean the Jews were caught up in their myth, as Eichmann was caught up in his myth, and Hitler in his, and these would never meet—because by and large the Jewish leaders, not only in Germany, were good liberals of the enlightenment tradition—gentlemen, aged gentlemen.

Ledeen: And therefore absolutely unable to deal with the reality of the . . .

Mosse: Well who could? Look at the story of Anne Frank.[40] What did the Franks do surrounded by the Nazis? They tried to live a normal middle-class life. Something that Bruno Bettleheim[41] already pointed out long ago and which was really absurd in these circumstances. They should have practiced fleeing and hiding better but they didn't. So the story of Anne Frank is really the story of a lasting middle-class myth in an extreme situation.

Ledeen: People are starting to point out that there is a kind of global responsibility for the final solution—that other countries could have taken Jews, others could have intervened, and so forth. There was an almost general silence about this subject wasn't there?

Mosse: Yes. At the time there was silence because people thought the war must have precedence—they didn't know what to do with all the Jews, and I think didn't really believe what was happening in spite of the growing evidence. The people who said it was happening were not believed. This can be illustrated through the attitude of Pius XII, which is not an unusual one. He said I'll be glad to condemn the murder of the Jews, but give me a white book as proof—that is a book of all the documents—and of course that was impossible. He also remained silent when the Roman Jews were rounded up under Nazi occupation. But the guilt is first of all with Hitler, the SS, and with all the collaborators. The others share perhaps a negative guilt, if you want to call it that. But I think the main guilt must not be diverted. Hitler is guilty, Himmler is guilty, Heydrich[42] is guilty—all the ones who took part, some of whom are only now coming to trial. The others are guilty by omission. But this is easier, you know, criticized in retrospect.

Ledeen: Now as you well know, many scholars—in particular political scientists — have attempted to put the analysis of fascism into a broader context and to deal with it as part of a more general phenomenon which they have called totalitarianism. What do you think of this methodology?

Mosse: I am opposed to the word totalitarianism because it seems to me an untrue generalization, or to put it better, it is a typical generalization from a liberal point of view. You will find that those who use "totalitarianism," let us say as the late Hannah Arendt did in her famous book *The Origins of Totalitarianism,*[43] put together everything that is opposed to liberal parliamentary and representative government. So they put into one pot communism, fascism, Stalin, and Hitler. This is one of the criticisms I have of the liberal point of view, because this point of view uses totalitarianism as a general catch phrase for anything that is antiliberal. But in reality it disguises the differences. There is a big difference between Lenin, Stalin, and Hitler. There is a big difference between bolshevism and fascism.

Ledeen: Then totalitarianism sums up all the governments we'd fought against in World War II and the Cold War.

Mosse: Yes. It is a typical Cold War phrase. It comes up in the Cold War in order to tar with the same brush everyone opposed to the so-called parliamentary democracies.

Ledeen: Let's just simply call them all the same thing.

Mosse: This does not mean, by the way, that Hannah Arendt's book does not have very fertile suggestions. She is the first one who said that it is important to investigate fascism as a mass movement. I do not have priority in that. Hannah Arendt's individual analyses are fruitful, but her overall concept is, I think, a product of the times in which she wrote.

Ledeen: In *The Origins of Totalitarianism* she gives great importance to something we haven't talked about very much, although we've touched on it from time to time, and that is the subject of terror in fascism, and national socialism. The terror was very important for the national socialist success, wasn't it?

Mosse: I think there is an evolution here. At first the terror was partly disguised and partly very episodic. Until 1936 there existed several concentration camps, but they weren't camps in which you remained, if you understand what I mean. The secret police was not fully formed until 1934. The terror that existed prior to, let us say, 1934-35 before the secret police really got going, was the terror of a successful movement which controlled the streets. There's always a certain terror there. The terror or oppression of all other political parties existed, of course—for example the arrests of communists, socialists, and republicans. All of these things are terror, but it wasn't as yet a mass terror so generalized that it would vitally affect the individual who would, in any case, be quite taken with much of national socialism and its success in getting rid of unemployment, its law and order, and its ideology. In other words, what Hannah Arendt and I mean by real mass terror was not necessary at first. The terror that was necessary at first was only terror against outspoken or, as they would say, inevitable enemies of the regime.

Ledeen: Kristalnacht?[44]

Mosse: Doesn't come till 1938. Don't let us confuse it. In the early years such mass terror wasn't necessary and because it wasn't necessary, except against the outspoken enemies of the regime, it could be instituted gradually. So it isn't as simple as just saying "terrorism." To sum up, at first you had mass terror by control of the streets, by the common enthusiasm, which is of course a terror against whoever disagreed with the consensus. There was individual terror only against the outspoken enemies of the regime, many of whom were allowed to flee the country. Some of them were put into concentration camps and were allowed to leave them again. The terror was tightened with the creation of a political police which stood outside the legal system. In fact I must stress that until 1937 the concentration camp system stood within the legal system. There were legal ways of getting people out of concentration camps until that time. But when, as we have said before, the tightening of the regime comes, from 1937 on, the terror becomes more general: universal spying is encouraged, the secret police becomes all pervasive, and to speak up, of course, meant martyrdom and destruction. This was a very shrewd and successful tactic on Hitler's part. It's very difficult to institute pervasive terror in a nation like Germany, but if you put people to sleep at the beginning they awake in a world of terror and it is too late.

You must look at it from this point of view because the only ones who were terrorized from the start were Jews and this was done through the tactic of provoking anti-Jewish riots before the Nuremberg laws, before every new step in Jewish policy. You can see that there was this kind of terror against the Jews, but not individual terror. The essence of terror is its impersonality. So I would say that as far as the Jews were concerned, much more important even than antisemitic riots was making myths come true: there was a department created in the Ministry of the Interior to unravel the universal world Jewish conspiracy. Such a conspiracy never existed. It came into existence by the fact that a bureaucracy worked on it. That is really what is important until 1937-38, when mass terror really starts.

But you mentioned the Crystal Night, when Hitler once again took an opportunity—that of the murder of an embassy attaché by a young Jew whose parents had been expelled from Germany—in order to signal a new turn in Jewish policy. This he did by giving Goebbels permission to loose terror against objects, not people, that is to say, to burn down synagogues and Jewish establishments. Himmler and Goering didn't want to do this because they wanted to preserve their future economic loot, but more important, they believed that such acts were ineffective. If you wanted to destroy the Jews it had to be done by "cold pogroms", as we call it—by bureaucracy. Well, in the end Hitler allowed Goebbels to set a signal for the Jews because the Jews themselves didn't want to emigrate. It was really a signal to the Jews of what was about to happen. After that, of course, he gave the Jewish question back to Goering and Himmler. Goering got his money (the

Jews had to pay for the damage), and economic Aryanization was instituted after that. Himmler got what he wanted—namely control of the emigration apparatus and eventually over the final solution. The Crystal Night is therefore an episode—and in many ways an atypical episode—in its individual violence. It was a sign, and Hitler liked to set signs. At the same time he made a very important speech in which he said that with my chief enemy I do not do battle: I first disarm him, I drive him into a corner, and then I put the rapier through his heart. And that is exactly how he proceeded on the Jewish question. He first isolated the Jews (one of the important landmarks here was the decision, taken in 1937-38, to deprive the Jewish religious community of its legal status), forced them into a corner, and then put a rapier through their hearts. Hitler not only set signs, but sometimes even talked in public, stating just how he was to proceed. For some reason not enough people listened to him, or believed him, or took him seriously.

Ledeen: Why did they consistently not believe Hitler's warnings and announcements?

Mosse: Well, there are two reasons. First of all, people cannot look into the future. When a leader of a nation says "this is my last territorial demand" after the occupation of the Rhineland or "my last act on the Jewish question" after the Nuremberg laws, people believe it because they cannot see that this is only a tactic and not true at all. But secondly, in these acts which point towards the final solution, nobody in Germany or anywhere in Europe would have believed that in twentieth-century Europe genocide was possible. We mustn't forget that. So that there is, after all, a certain resistance to such a belief; there was still a concept of civilization, of culture, of the country of Goethe and

Mozart, and all that sort of thing. I come back here to something Hannah Arendt did not understand in *Eichmann in Jerusalem* about which we have already talked—that Hitler had his myths and others had their myths, and the latter were the myths of a civilized continent of Europe, replete with middle-class values, with decency, with being a gentleman—and of course that played directly into Hitler's hands.

Ledeen: Now, we've spoken about national socialism, about the roots of national socialism, about the development, to a certain extent, of the national socialist regime. Before we get into the subject of fascism in general, the points of contact between fascism and national socialism, I'd just like to ask you briefly a couple of questions about World War II itself. What do you think about A.J.P. Taylor's thesis[45] concerning World War II? To what extent is it a planned result of Hitler's mind and to what extent is it a result of circumstances and accident?

Mosse: The answer is that it is both. Taylor is right on one level—that Hitler did not plan the actual date of the outbreak of World War II, that if he could have gotten the territory he wanted without war, undoubtedly he would have taken it without war. On the other hand, ever since 1937 and his speech to the generals, the so-called Hossbach protocols, it's quite clear that Hitler envisaged a war as inevitable, that he prepared for it as inevitable, and the fact that he believed that such a war must come sooner or later does not contradict the fact that he didn't put an exact date on it.

Ledeen: So, he was ready for war in a general sort of way, but when it would happen depended upon circumstances.

Mosse: Yes. He believed, for example, that Great Britain would not follow through with its guarantee for Poland.

Ledeen: While we're on the subject of war itself, many people have suggested that part of the reason for the failure of the war effort by the Germans was due to the racial policy and ideology. Hitler is said to have thought that the Slavs were inferior and therefore refused to believe the testimony of some of his generals that the Russians were fighting very well, were putting up stiff resistance, and so forth. Similarly, there was a great deal of diversion of men and supplies to the camps instead of sending them to the front, and this cost the Nazis heavily.

Mosse: There is no doubt that World War II brings out the decisive element of race in national socialist thought. Most decisive perhaps in the end was Hitler's rejection of what he called Jewish physics — that is to say, all of modern physics, which retarded the making of an atom bomb. There is quite a lot of internal correspondence about this. If Hitler had early on given his approval to the construction of an atom bomb and had overcome his hatred of what he called Jewish physics, then maybe the war would have had a different ending. So I think this is very crucial. You're quite right that to a certain extent the diversion of transport to the concentration and extermination camps hindered the war, as did the ghetto rebellions, but I think these were not such serious hindrances to victory as the matter of the bomb. I would add to that as well the internal dispute of how to invade Russia. Alfred Rosenberg[46]— certainly a racist in any sense of the word — proposed that the German armies come to Russia as liberators—that the Russians not be enslaved again but that they be given a certain autonomy. This was rejected. There were many signs that if the Germans had come to Russia as liberators not only from Soviet rule but also as the liberators of the Russian nationalities, they might have had a great deal of local support. But once it was clear that they came to Russia as enslavers, the matter was entirely different. That is really the important matter — that and the bomb, rather than the transport needed for camps or the troops needed for the ghetto rebellions.

Ledeen: I also had another point in mind. If one reads, for example, Guderian's[47] letters to Hitler shortly after the invasion of Russia, he writes back to Hitler and says that the Russians are fighting extremely well and that it's going to be a very long and difficult battle. And Hitler replied, "don't tell me this nonsense about Slavs fighting well. Slavs can't fight well at all."

Mosse: Well, that's true, of course, But in the last resort what really defeated the Nazis were considerations of strategy and the Russian winter. That proved to be decisive.

Ledeen: And in the end, when the war is hopelessly compromised and the Russians are advancing on one front and the allies on the other, it is true that Hitler develops this kind of death wish for the German people, isn't it? That he develops the attitude, they have demonstrated that they were unworthy of me, so let them all die now in this final battle.

Mosse: They were unworthy of their destiny, as Hitler would have put it, and so Germany has to be destroyed together with all of Europe. Yes, certainly. He issued orders for such destruction which were not carried out. It's quite clear that Hitler could not face the defeat. He didn't believe in the defeat, not even when the Russians were already in Berlin. There was always the belief in the mystery weapon, the new mystery weapon which would bring success but which, thanks to Hitler, was started too late to bring that success. So that, in the end, only destruction and suicide remained. But we must be careful to distinguish the last phase from the earlier phases of World War II. In the earlier phases Hitler's strategy and tactics were very effective, and it is only when the Soviet offensive and the allied offensive were having success that Hitler really lost contact with reality, and never totally. I've said earlier that Hitler's success was due to this mixture of myth and reality in his character; but in the end it was the myth which triumphed.

Chapter Five

Ledeen: Let's turn now to the discussion of fascism in general. The first question is, do you think there is a fascism in general or do we have to talk about particular national phenomena between World Wars I and II?

Mosse: I think there is a fascism in general, but I think this fascism must be discussed within the national context.

Ledeen: Would you like to elaborate on that a little bit? What is it? Is it possible to say what this fascism in general is?

Mosse: Yes, I think so. Everywhere after 1918 there was a tendency in Europe for what we might call a radicalism of the Right—a radicalism that went beyond conservatism, that posited a certain revolution. What sort of a revolution? I think that we find that it is a revolution of the spirit which was supposed to have concrete consequences. That is to say, this radicalism of the Right wanted to do away with the traditional hierarchial structures of the society and of the state. It did not want to abolish the state, but to substitute instead hierarchies based on function rather than on status. Together with that they wanted hierarchies based on an allegiance to the national mystique, which in Germany meant to race. And through that a new man would come about—a man who would symbolize these new hierarchies and who, through his own force of will, would make everything come out all right. Moreover, I must say, in all of fascism we find this combination of looking backwards to the national mystique (in Germany and Austria, to the racial mystique)—and at the same time forward to the war, to the new race of heroes which came from the war. And this was always combined with a support for what were called national values, but which were in reality generally accepted middle-class values—that is honest labor, loyalty, cleanliness, productivity, etc. The idea was, I think, wherever fascism existed that these values would solve all political and economic problems and therefore fascism never had a very definite political or economic stance. It was thought in Germany that if the Aryan came to power—elsewhere if the proper national mystique broke through—all problems would be automatically solved. I should also, of course, mention that all fascisms were mass movements—another reason why conservatives hated them so much. So there are enough things in common to *all* fascism that I think you must say there is such a phenomenon as fascism and that within that phenomenon there are variations. Perhaps I should also add while I think of it, that all fascism—more than any other revolutionary impetus between the wars—stressed the idea of community. The idea of leadership (which we already discussed) came out of the idea community—a community of affinity, not an enforced community; the kind of longing for *camaraderie* which came from the war. It's very important—not only the idea of struggle which comes from the war, but the idea of *camaraderie*.

Ledeen: You see this as unique to fascism? Isn't it common also in the left-wing movements following the war?

Mosse: No. There is a certain overlap in Germany. There is a kind of socialist-Volkish ideology which you have above all in the revolution in Bavaria with Gustav Landauer[48] and people like that. But I would say in reality that socialism contains much too much reason, didacticism, and education. Moreover, the revolution of the Left had a definite economic theory—it believed that the way to get revolution is to raise revolutionary consciousness through education, through an appeal to reason rather than through an appeal to the national mystique or emotion. I think there is a very great difference, though at times (as I said, in the Bavarian revolution, for example) they perhaps come closer together, but never *that* close together. I would make a very definite distinction here between the revolution of the Left and the revolution of the Right.

Ledeen: If we can summarize what you just said about the revolution of the Right, you see it as an attempt to substitute new kinds of hierarchies for the old ones. In Germany these hierarchies are tied to Volkish and racist principles.

Mosse: In Germany this is true, but elsewhere they are always tied to national mystique of one sort or another.

Ledeen: Yes. And in Italy for example.

Mosse: Romanità.

Ledeen: I must say you don't find this at the beginning

of Italian fascism. You find it for the most part much later. But there is the so-called generation of the trenches in fascism.

Mosse: It is always related somehow to nationalistic feelings.

Ledeen: Yes, but do you think that the new hierarchies in Italian and German fascism are really so similar when you look at them? After all, the Germans are speaking of a "new man" who was not so much created by World War I as he had been so to speak liberated by the war; whereas in the Italian view the new fascist man — and this will remain true all the way through Italian fascism—was always something that had to be created, not something that was already there.

Mosse: Well as I said earlier there were these two trends—the SS certainly thought the new man had to be created, but I think in the end the two men are not that dissimilar. Both stress, above all, creativity—they're creative people—because all fascism has within it an element of poetry, as Brasillach[49] in France rightly said. That is to say they stress a myth of creativity as over against liberalism and positivism. To a very large extent the new man was a stereotype based on the war and on certain ideas of beauty which D'Annunzio and the Germans had in common—the idea of classical beauty and beauty as a principle of order. So that here again there is a great similarity. Moreover, the two men are also leadership types. That is to say, leadership ideas of *camarderie* and community are also held in common. In other words, this new man is not a leader because in some way he's been born a leader, but rather he becomes a leader because he is better than others. It is this storm-trooper idea from the war which is common to D'Annunzio and to Jünger. So I would say that the new fascist man in Italy and in Germany has certain things in common. The new man in the fascist movement in the Balkans—the Iron Guard for example—is a little different because there Christian elements played an important role. The new man in the Iron Guard is a believing Christian. I should perhaps add one other thing: all these are youths. Youth is worshipped. This is after all really new. You don't get this worship of youth until the 1880s, so fascism builds on that. But socialism does not build on that.

Ledeen: I would just caution about confusing D'Annunzio's vision of the new man with fascism's vision of the new man because in many ways they are very different. In this I think D'Annunzio is not really a fascist.

Mosse: There are common aspects to this vision of the new man—they have certain common sources such as the search for an elan at the end of the century. Of course, the German new man has an additional source which I think only becomes important later in D'Annunzio's life—namely Wagner. That is extremely important because the new man of, let us say, Bergson and Nietzsche has a kind of uncontrolled dynamic, but the whole essence of Wagner, as Hitler and many others say it, was to tame the new man into a certain historical and racial setting. Wagner's heroes, or Wagner's new men, if you like, were no longer the kind of new man like Zarathustra, but were instead ancient German heroes dressed up in sentimentalized and middle-class garb.

Ledeen: Yes, I entirely agree with that.

Mosse: But of course D'Annunzio became fascinated with this later in life when he bought Wagner's house. Moreover, I think it is quite clear that another element in common (and yet different according to national context) is this matter of alienation. All fascism promises an end to alienation and indeed Hitler had a very startling passage in *Mein Kampf* where he says that when a man comes out of his factory and into a mass movement he becomes a part of a community and ends his alienation. But what is of course different are aspects of the idea of the community. D'Annunzio's concern in Fiume for the oppressed nations, for example, would be unthinkable for the Nazis. They despised oppressed nations because they were weak and degenerate and had to be ruled by the Aryans, by the new racial heroes. To give only one example: Hitler believed that when the Aryans had emigrated from India to Europe they left behind in India a degenerate race so that the white man had to rule India. Hitler supported British imperialism, and simply wanted to substitute German for British imperialism. This also seems to me an important point.

Ledeen: Can we go back to the alienation problem for just a second? I think what you've said is terribly important, and I'm sure that Mussolini would have agreed with Hitler that man overcomes his sense of alienation in the modern world by his participation in a mass movement. There is no question but that D'Annunzio at Fiume discovered and perfected this kind of form of mass participation which does indeed overcome alienation. I would only want to point out on the political side for D'Annunzio that in the constitution of Fiume—in the *Carta del Carnaro*— he did take a more radical position, which was that man would overcome his alienation through his work and not simply through participation in a mass.

Mosse: Yes, but there again all fascism stressed work. All fascism put itself up as a theory of production that derived from the nineteenth century and was a French contribution to later fascist theory. French socialists like Proudhon in the early nineteenth century or Drumont[50] at the turn of the twentieth century stressed productivity through work. They have been called national socialists, for they believed in the mystique of the nation which provided the proper community and opposed finance capital. This applied, of course, to Drumont more than Proudhon who opposed private property, though both saw the Jew as unproductive — as the finance capitalist — and therefore as the enemy who had to be destroyed. The enemy of fascism is always characterized as one who does not work, as one who does not know the dignity of work, as one who is opposed to production.

I want to come back to this a little later but there is another point I want to make here. Hitler, D'Annunzio, and Mussolini believed that the community climaxes in the nation, but to D'Annunzio and Mussolini this community is the state not the *volk* or the race. The result of this must not be overlooked. It would be quite impossible to envisage in Italian fascism, for example, what was to have been the final result of the victory of German national socialism—namely the promise by Hitler to Himmler and the SS of the totally non-German territory of Burgundy from which the SS would rule Europe as a supranational elite, a supranational order of racial chivalry. This became reality to a certain extent in another institution which you do not find at all in Fascist Italy: the International Brigades of the SS which, like the French Brigade Charlemagne, were truly international armies based not on national but on racial criteria. The Italian brand of fascism stays within the framework of the nation and the state; national socialism goes outside the framework as a result of its racial ideas.

Ledeen: I think it is significant along the lines of what you were saying that Italian, Spanish, and French fascism are by and large national fascisms and remain such. Even when Mussolini develops for a short time a theory of international fascism it will still be an international of national fascism, so to speak. But Hitler doesn't have this. For Hitler it's just one big national socialism, one big Reich.

Mosse: Ruled by Aryans. The French intellectual fascists were much closer in that to Hitler than they were to Mussolini. In the end many joined the Charlemagne Brigade and found their home, as it were, in an international racial elite.

Ledeen: Whom are we speaking of here?

Mosse: Drieu La Rochelle, De La Mazière[51] whose book about the Charlemagne Brigade *The Captive Dreamer,* you might have seen, and those like Brasillach who did not join Charlemagne but dreamt of joining it. All the fascist intellectuals did dream of such an international Europe—racial Europe—if you like. Indeed that was one of the attractions of national socialism to French intellectuals.

Ledeen: We've spoken a good deal about the Nazi revolution and the revolution of the Right. To what extent do you think there are traditional European revolutionary elements in national socialism or in fascism in general? To put it a little differently, it's been suggested recently[52] that there is a component of Italian fascism which is linked to the French Revolution and in particular to the revolutionary vision of Rousseau. This is implied in the Talmon thesis[53] that the French Revolution led to a totalitarian democracy.

Mosse: This is not a simple question to answer. I think none of fascism really took the French Revolution as the paradigm of revolutions. There was very little in fascism of storming the Bastille. I think we must put it on a different level. There was a great deal of Jacobinism in all of fascism, especially of course in French fascism, where you can trace it directly to the Jacobin revival of the Paris Commune of 1870. But I think this is true everywhere. I agree with the Talmon thesis, on the level that the French Revolution was a dress rehearsal for modern mass movements—for modern secular symbolisms—and that the Enlightenment had a problem within it which was its abstraction—its abstract nature. As a reaction Rousseau called for various symbols which would make it concrete—the national monuments, the goddess of reason and all of this. About the Enlightenment I think there are two points of view possible, both of which are actually correct. There is the view of Peter Gay[54] which looks at the Enlightenment from within. What the philosophers actually wanted was the predominance of the critical mind. From that point of view, they were in no way the ancestors of authoritarianism. But there is the other side, what I call the darker side of the Enlightenment (which in addition to Talmon, also the Germans of the so-called Frankfurt school, Horckheimer and Adorno pointed out)—namely the Enlightenment as depersonalization because of its abstract theories, its intellectualism. This depersonalization became in fact a forerunner of modern positivism, producing the first racial classification. That is another side of the Enlightenment. But this side called for Rousseau's patriotic ceremony, a certain romanticism, and a certain attempt to personalize the depersonalized. We can look at all of fascism as an attempt to personalize the abstract. That is in my opinion the connection with the French Revolution and the Enlightenment.

Ledeen: There is the one you stress in your book which is the idea of national festival.

Mosse: Well that is making the abstract personal. You substitute a goddess of reason for the Virgin Mary.

Ledeen: Yes and then you write a letter to the king of Poland saying what Poland needs is an annual festival.

Mosse: Exactly, a patriotic festival around a national monument. It's no coincidence that national monuments as national symbols come out of the eighteenth century.

Ledeen: So you would agree with De Felice when he says there is this Jacobin element in fascism, that there is a kind of spurious revolutionary element.

Mosse: I would say that as the Jacobins were, as a matter of fact, the first middle-class revolutionaries, and we are dealing with fascism at least in central and perhaps in southern Europe as a middle-class phenomenon, this is true.

Ledeen: Is fascism then a middle-class revolution?

Mosse: In certain countries, yes. Certainly I would say in Germany. It was, as I said before, an attempt to keep middle-class values intact. So for Hitler there can be no question that it was a middle-class revolution. For

Mussolini, I am not sure. In France it becomes a kind of Nietzschean ecstasy much more than a middle-class revolution, but as most French fascists were an intellectual coterie it's a different matter.

Ledeen: It probably isn't fair to compare movements with regimes.

Mosse: That's true except that the regimes were inherent in the movement. You can also make too big a difference because, though the movement in power changed—became more respectable, had more trouble with the activism from the beginning and tried to defeat it—there are still continuities. I wouldn't make the break all that sharp myself, at least not in Germany. And in France, Rumania, and Hungary where fascism never came to power, I would say the difference is that their fascism could keep the activism intact, you see?

Ledeen: What do you think of the viability of the distinction between racist and non-racist fascisms, that is a kind of neonazism that would cover Germany, Austria, Rumania perhaps, and some of the other Eastern European fascisms and the kind of, for lack of a better word, humanist Latin fascism that would deal with Spain, Italy, France, and so forth?

Mosse: Well, I would not say "humanist fascism" but certainly this becomes extremely important not just for the Jews but for the dynamic of the movement. Racism deepened certain elements of fascist aggression and fascist dynamic. Now, racist fascism comes wherever there are such traditions in the past. We have again the problem that without tradition you cannot activate anything. So as Italy had no real antisemitic tradition, there was really nothing there to activate for fascism.

Ledeen: When the racial laws were passed they were treated with much disrespect.

Mosse: Well of course. In Spain they had an old racial tradition, and how!, dating from the sixteenth century. But there were no longer any Jews in Spain. Subsequently it was totally irrelevant. You also do not get racial traditions in countries where there is more than one nationality. So that for example at the beginning the Rexists, the fascist movement in Belgium, repudiated ideas of race. One was Flemish or Walloon. Similarly Mussert, the National Socialist leader in Holland, was ambivalent on race. All of these movements of course became racist in the end under German influence. In the Balkans, however, it is a more difficult matter. Take the Iron Guard. The Iron Guard was violently antisemitic because in those regions the Jews were literally the middle class. They were extremely exposed, and the hostility was correspondingly great. Indeed, the last leader of the Iron Guard, Horia Sima, published a book two years ago in Argentina — a book in which he repeats everything about the Jewish-Bolshevik-capitalist conspiracy. Just as Léon Degrelle, the leader of the Rexists published, I think, perhaps about ten years ago, a totally unrepentant and violent memoir in his exile in Spain. But these movements in the Balkans were militantly Christian. Here the matter of conversion was bothersome. For example, it is claimed that Codreanu, the first leader of the Iron Guard, was married by a priest who was a converted Jew. I do not know the actual truth of this statement but certainly it was always a problem here as it was not in central Europe, for example. So it isn't very easy but I would say as a general rule that you get racist fascism wherever there was a lively antisemitic tradition and wherever there were Jews who were visible either as revolutionaries (and very often they were) or as leaders in financial capitalism (which is after all the only capitalism fascism ever opposed) and who were visible in cultural affairs as well. So where there were no Jews visible in this particular manner, fascism wasn't particularly racist. But even if all these conditions are present, it doesn't mean you have to have a racist fascism. France is an example.

Ledeen: And Italy.

Mosse: Jews were not very visible in Italy in that sense. They were not revolutionaries.

Ledeen: Sure they were. In the socialist party—Modigliani, Treves and . . .

Mosse: Yes, but nothing to compare to leaders like Béla Kun, Kurt Eisner, or Rosa Luxemburg who actually led revolutions. Nor did they dominate culture as, let us say, the Jews in Germany in fact dominated a certain culture; at least that culture which everybody thought was the culture of the Weimar intellectuals. It's not quite the same. France is more relevant I think. There racism did not make a breakthrough, even though France had a very viable antisemitic tradition.

Ledeen: Do you think it might have something to do with the numbers of Jews? In both France and Italy they were really dealing with tiny numbers of Jews whereas in Germany, Austria and so forth they were dealing with great numbers of them?

Mosse: No, I don't think it has to do with numbers of Jews. It has to do with their visibility—everywhere—Paris had its ghetto, the Marais, London had its Whitechapel, and Berlin had the Grenadierstrasse. These were the only ghettos in those towns. So the

Jews in all these countries were visible, visible as a different tribe; visible in politics and culture. But I think it almost has to be a combination of these things.

Ledeen: You agree then that it is important to make a distinction between racist fascism and nonracist fascism. The question is, at what point do the differences between these two threaten to obliterate the possibility of talking about a fascism in general?

Mosse: Oh, I don't think they obliterate that because basically, as I said before, the definition I have given of the revolution of the Right is common to all of them. This, though racism gave a greater dynamic—a greater energy if you like—to the fascisms which had it, was crucial for the Jews. I do not think this defeats a common definition.

Ledeen: Well what do you make then of the early antagonism and apparently very strong antagonism between Hitler and Mussolini? Particularly the fact that Mussolini thought that Hitler was a mad man because of the racial ideas.

Mosse: Hitler was puzzled and never understood why Mussolini did not institute racial policies in the first place. He never understood why the racial laws were not properly enforced. You've got two totally different men. After all, Mussolini was a man of the world, a journalist who had gotten around, who had already been a leader in another kind of political movement while Hitler was a man of the provinces, profoundly narrow, who had never really left the German-speaking world. While Mussolini had a great deal of cynicism, Hitler had none, as we have already seen. So the gulf between them could not have been wider. But I don't think personal differences should obliterate the factors that were in common because when all is said and done Hitler revered Mussolini. Mussolini was probably the only person to whom Hitler had the deepest loyalty. With all the dispute about German national socialism and its relation to Italian fascism, that factor must not be forgotten, at least from Hitler's side.

Ledeen: But, on the other hand there is a profound ideological difference between the two men, isn't there? That is the question of the nature of the nation.

Mosse: There was certainly a great difference—which comes from the difference and the traditions of their nations—but there are also similarities—the similarities which come from World War I. Both Italy and Germany proceeded by inducing, if you like, a civil war situation. They manifest the similar problems of activism, law and order, and a mass movement of the Right. All of these are certainly there—with all the differences. And the differences I think come from the quite different national histories. I wouldn't minimize the differences, but I would not make them total, either. Both were after all authoritarian states. Both were states where the leader was all important— as a symbol and a manager if you like—Hitler perhaps more active than Mussolini. Mussolini more a manager type; Hitler more a didactic leader type, but still there is a lot in common.

Ledeen: I think there may be one fundamental differ- ence between national socialism and Italian fascism that we haven't dealt with yet (though we have dealt with it obliquely a couple of times), and that is the difference that stems from their divergent views of human nature. The Nazi view of human nature is, after all, fundamentally a static one. The Nazi man, the

Aryan man, the SS to the contrary notwithstanding, comes more or less fully formed. For the fascists, on the other hand, there was an act of creation set for sometime in the future. There was still work to be done on the human material.

Mosse: I have stressed the similarities—such similarities as there were—but this is an important difference: that whatever one can say about the regimes, the results of the war, the longing for camaraderie, all of those matters which Professor De-Felice for example, in his volume[55] has said also apply to Italy, there are the differences in human nature which stem from the difference of national tradition. Italian nationalism is a Mazzinian nationalism. It has a great deal of humanity in it—it is open-ended. You do not find this in Nazi Germany at all. Since the racial view of man forecloses it, it narrows evermore the definition of man until the only true man is the Aryan. If we take the Nazi definition, the one who has at least three Aryan grandparents is an Aryan. Now to an Italian this would seem ridiculous, but not to all Italians. Not to Farinacci[56], Preziosi[57], Evola[58]. But to a great many—to most Italians, with few exceptions—it seemed utterly ridiculous because there is no base in Italian tradition for this kind of view. When Italian racism was introduced, it had to be invented and you get a crude transposition from the German Aryan man to the Mediterranean Aryan man, whatever that was supposed to mean. As I have said all along you need tradition to activate thought or else it can not be activated. This is without any question a very fundamental difference.

Ledeen: Well also the fact that Italian fascism with all its authoritarianism, or presumed totalitarianism, (which undoubtedly existed), was still a confessional state.

There was still the Concordat. The Pope was present. The Church.

Mosse: There were more differences. It isn't only the Church. True fascism was set in a Catholic country, but there was also the king, there was also the senate, there was also Croce. Now all of this was, of course, totally impossible in Germany. There, Hitler had control of the state and the party. Mussolini never had full control of the state. So there's a difference here which I do not mean to minimize. But there is another difference which I think is very important, and which really typifies all the other differences. Germany had no antifascism and Italy did—and a very large and important antifascist movement. Now why should it have been so? I suggest there are two reasons: one is of course that Italian fascism lasted so much longer that there could be an antifascist movement.

Ledeen: Well, still it developed early.

Mosse: Yes, it developed early, but that is not a very satisfactory explanation. The answer is really in the different national traditions. National socialism was so total a world view—so total a commitment—and rested at the beginning on so total a consensus that no antifascism, apart from small groups, ever existed. Of course you come here to German history again. In German history there is no great tradition of resistance in the first place.

Ledeen: Well it's an occupier and not an occupied nation.

Mosse: Well I wouldn't even say that. It didn't occupy much in the nineteenth century and Italy, after all, occupied as well, so I wouldn't say that necessarily. But

I would say it is a much denser kind of nationalism—a much more restrictive kind of nationalism. Let me put it a different way. In Germany, Austria, and to a certain extent in Eastern Europe, racism allied itself with all the factors of the nineteenth century. It allied itself with nationalism, with middle-class morality, and with expansionism. Racism allied itself with science, with everything. So that when it came to activate a mass movement based on racist principles, racism was so diffused that it could make a total claim. Now in Italy racism never allied itself with anything. There's a great difference.

Ledeen: It's peculiar, isn't it? Because on the one hand the two fascisms which come to power both come to power in countries where national unification came late in the nineteenth century, and on the other hand, these two nationalisms, despite their late blooming, are very different.

Mosse: Yes, yes, but that's not surprising because every nationalism in Europe is different. I would say it this way: that there is a common kind of national tradition or tradition of national liberation in Central and Eastern Europe. It is here that Herder[59] was really important. In Eastern Europe nationalism by and large received a great deal of its stimulus from Germany and German nationalism. But this is not true for Italy, which received some stimulus from German nationalism but by no means to the extent, let us say, of Eastern Europe.

Ledeen: Really, there are not only two different concepts of nationalism involved, but there are also two different concepts of national leadership, aren't there? There is no *duce principio* as there is a *Führer Prinzip.* Hitler is, so to speak, above even the state. The SS

swore a direct oath of loyalty to Hitler and not to
Germany.

Mosse: Yes, that's correct, that's quite correct.

Ledeen: Something like this would be unthinkable in
Italy.

Mosse: Yes, but on the other hand we mustn't exaggerate this. Hitler was not *above* the state, he *was* the state.
In other words we must come back to this matter—that
the actual leadership philosophy was not so different, I
think, in Italy and in Germany. The leader was *primus
inter pares.* Whatever else you might say there was no
idea of divine right kingship; it came out of this idea of
community which we have discussed already. The
leader wasn't enthroned above the masses, he just did
everything better. And as I very well remember, you
had Mussolini as the harvester, Mussolini as the build-
er, Mussolini as the jogger, Mussolini as the
sportsman. Well Hitler did much less of this, as a
matter of fact, but there was a common element. And
Hitler never was photographed as Mussolini was,
barebreasted and harvesting. That wouldn't have been
in character at all.

Ledeen: Kissing babies?

Mosse: He kissed babies. The idea was that he was not a
superman but a better man. The Aryan symbol, not
above the Aryan. If there really was a difference it was
a difference of national character. Let me tell you a
story which perhaps better illustrates it than any great
historical analyses. I remember in 1936 riding in a
train from Florence to Rome and every train had a
carabiniere on it with a machine gun. The people in
my compartment were telling anti-Mussolini jokes.

The carabiniere of course walked up and down the train corridor and I, coming from a German ambience, was terrified. But what happened in the end was that the carabiniere came into the compartment, not to arrest us, but to tell other Mussolini jokes. Now such a people is very difficult to govern in an authoritarian way. I should think that Italians are very difficult to govern either for fascists or for people's republics. I do not think they are destined for that sort of thing by tradition. Such an episode could never have happened in Germany.

Ledeen: Wasn't there the joke about Hitler, Goering, and Goebbels on the Rhine, the boat sank and Germany was saved?

Mosse: But these jokes were told secretly. They were whispered.

Ledeen: To get back to the leadership idea. Mussolini is a leader and in the popular literature comes to represent a new man of the sort that does not yet exist in Italy. He is not first among equals, he is the first among the new men—he is first among a new breed. He's taken always as a model of what Italians are to become, but he is not taken very often as an example of what Italians are.

Mosse: Well, still there was a certain attempt to fasten on to Roman models and the whole worship of archeology, so I think it's not only looking to the future. There is also always an element of the Roman past. But I think you are quite correct; there is more open-endedness in Italy than in Germany, and the difference is certainly in the concept of race. Race is always likened to a tree, it doesn't change. The roots of the race are always the same. And all you have are the

branches and the crown of a tree. We might as well use
the image that the Nazis themselves used. The Dar-
winist element which is stressed by many historians of
national socialism is simply projected onto a struggle
of the race with its enemies. There is no natural selection. The natural selection has already taken place
with the birth of the race. That I think is *very* important. One must not call Nazism social Darwinism.

Ledeen: Yes, I entirely agree with that. I think it is very
important. We've spoken a lot about the theory of
national socialism and about the ideology which you
see lying at the base of all of fascism. Could you say
something about the structures of national socialism
and of fascism? Do you see an underlying similarity, or
are there over-riding differences?

Mosse: There are both similarities and important differences. The similarity is that in all fascist regimes the
structure centered around various leaders and their
followers. They all had what Robert Koehl[60] called a
"feudal structure" in that regard. But the difference
between Germany and Italy is significant. In Italy
these leaders and their followers had a territorial base.
They were the "RAS"—the provincial bosses. Well that
did not exist in Germany where Hitler abolished the
individual states, and so centralized from the beginning. The power base of the leaders lay elsewhere. It
lay with Himmler in the SS, or it lay in the labor
front—in other words it lay partly in national organizations and partly in whether or not the leaders could
get Hitler's ear. In the centralization of power Hitler
himself seems to have played a larger part than Mussolini. In Germany there could not have been a fascist
grand council which might overthrow the leader. National socialism could never have ended as did Italian
fascism. That is of course a very great difference to-

gether with that other difference of the importance of the state, the difference in the legal structure. I must issue a word of warning here that until 1937 even in national socialist Germany the existing legal structures still played a role. They played less of a role after that, of course.

Perhaps we should summarize the structure of national socialism by saying that in all matters—in foreign policy, in Jewish policy, in the tightening up of the terror—the crucial incision comes in 1938. It is then that much which was inherent in the regime becomes public, is spelled out and becomes enforced. After the winter 1937/38, for example, there's a flood of ordinances on the Jewish question, such as there hardly was before. And yet I think we must also say that the signs had already been there, not only in *Mein Kampf,* but in the racial measures. I've said earlier that in the Nuremberg laws, Hitler chose the most moderate of four proposals submitted to him. But side by side with the Nuremberg laws ran the law for the prevention of hereditarily diseased offspring which by 1935 had already led to forced sterilization. That was already a sign in the wind that the Nazis took racism seriously, except that the tactics of Hitler were so confusing that people didn't pay any attention. There were a lot of people who thought that with the coming to power the Nazis had abandoned their racial ideas, modified them, or become respectable, but that just didn't happen.

Chapter Six

Ledeen: It must be said that most of what we have been talking about here when we have discussed the question of fascism has tended toward a cultural interpretation of the phenomenon.

Mosse: I am very glad you brought this up because I have often been accused of this and too little attention has been paid here to what is meant by culture. We have not been discussing fascism as a cultural phenomenon in the oldfashioned sense of culture as having to do, let us say, solely with literature, with art, but rather as culture as an attitude of mind—we have really been talking about fascism as an attitude of mind. Now this is very important because this is again something common to *all* fascism. All fascisms rejected classical political theory. That is why Anglo-Saxon scholars have such a difficult time discussing it. They're always looking for logical, consistent political theories. But fascism regarded itself, always, wherever it was, as an attitude of mind, an attitude towards life. And I take this seriously. When I am accused of making a cultural interpretation of fascism, I say all right. Let us take fascism as an attitude of mind—as a myth by which people define themselves and their place in the world. But then let us also say that this myth, this attitude of mind, connects to reality because it functions within a social and economic context. So that when you say we have been making a cultural interpretation of fascism what I really mean by that is again a dialectic between peoples' vision of their place in the universe and the reality within which they live.

This, by the way, would be the true Marxist approach which must be based on a dialectic and cannot be based on a unicausal approach, i.e. *all* economics, *all* politics, *all* social class. That is a static approach. It ignores the essence of Marxism—namely its Hegelian ingredient, its dynamic, its dialectic.

Ledeen: Yes, but on the other hand we should mention another contrast between Italy and Germany. We should say something about the class basis for fascism. We've said that in Germany by and large, we were talking about a middle-class movement.

Mosse: Well, I have difficulty with that. We must distinguish here the meaning of class. There is an economic and social meaning of class which we all know—working class, middle class, upper class. But there is also class as value. Now fascism everywhere annexed middle-class values. Middle-class values have become cross-class values by 1918—long before that. But I think you mean class in a purely economic and social sense.

Ledeen: I was talking about class in terms of where the support for fascism comes from. Who votes fascist, who takes out fascist party membership? Who are they?

Mosse: I am very skeptical of making an analysis of

national socialism on the basis of election statistics. This has become very fashionable, but I think it is very dangerous. An antiparliamentary party is a party in which many sympathizers never vote, so election statistics never tell the whole story. Membership statistics are also very difficult in national socialism because until the 1930s people passed through it, going from one party to another. Membership in these parties was very unstable.

Ledeen: One of the latest results of the analysis of Nazi election returns[61] in the late '20s and early '30s supports in a surprising and very unexpected way something that DeFelice said about Italian fascism, namely that a lot of the support for national socialism seems to have come from people who are newly arrived in the political process—that they are not people, so to speak, who have become alienated from other political parties and have turned to the Nazis, but they are people who have been mobilized politically for the first time.

Mosse: There's no question but that is correct. For one thing we've said it's a youth party so you mustn't forget those youths who first came to vote. This becomes very important, and I would say that everywhere fascism is a process of political mobilization. It is most effective where there are no socialist parties, but even where there are socialist parties it mobilizes certain strata of the population which were not co-opted by the socialist parties, not to mention the centrist parties. And these strata take in a great many classes in Germany, except for the upper classes and the nobility, the big industrialists, and the majority of the working classes. I think these classes were not really encompassed, but everything in between was encompassed in one way or another: the professional class—the teachers, and above all the elementary school teachers—for example, who were teachers who had very little status and who thought they should have more. Similarly quite respectable middle-class people—retail shopowners, smaller merchants, some skilled workers, master craftsmen—were all encompassed by Nazism.

Ledeen: I am surprised to hear you say that the fascist political mobilization was most effective in areas where there were no socialist parties because one of the major theses of traditional historiography is that fascism is fundamentally an antisocialist and anticommunist movement.

Mosse: No, no. This is again a matter of *fact* not a matter of speculation. I have already said that in Rumania where you have peasant and working-class fascism or in Argentina, Peronism, and Hungary where you have working-class fascism there was no prior mobilization by Marxist parties. Again this is not my own thesis. This is Juan Linz's thesis, which I find corresponds to the facts of the situation.

I should add here that there is a controversy over whether national socialism was only a mirror, as it were, of Marxism—a counter movement—or whether it stood on its own feet. Ernst Nolte argued that it was a mirror counter movement, but I do not think this is correct. There was a separate nationalist tradition, a separate racist tradition, a separate tradition of the kind of values which fascism annexed. It was much more than just a mirror image of Marxism.

Ledeen: More than just an antimovement.

Mosse: Yes. There is no question about that. We are now in the same kind of mistaken analysis which the liberals make who think it is simply an antiparliamentary movement. But it is not simply either an antiparliamentary movement or an anti-Marxist movement. It is all of that, but beyond that it has its own liturgy and attitude towards life. Some parts of it are borrowed from Marxist practice, such as the May Day parade and the red colors in the Nazi flag. These are borrowed from the workers' movement. But when it became a synthesis for its followers, it was something positive in its own right and not just merely an antimovement.

Ledeen: This then brings us logically to the question of the role of the leaders and the poetry of fascism. We've talked about this indirectly several times. There is, for example, Brasilach's famous phrase that Hitler and Mussolini were poets of revolution. What is the truth of this statement?

Mosse: The truth of the statement is that fascism and national socialism, having a great talent for mass movement, combine politics and aesthetics. Politics and aesthetics are always combined as long as men think in stereotypes, as long as ideas of beauty and ugliness are so important in people's lives that they become political categories. Thus the beauty of the national symbols which always went back to a classical tradition in Germany or to a romantic tradition. People had very definite ideas of what was beautiful and what was ugly, and of course racism made an alliance with beauty and defined ugliness in its own terms. So what we have there is that in modern mass politics aesthetics plays a very great part because politics must be defined as attitudes towards life. It becomes a total. The difference after all between liberal politics and fascist or socialist politics is that liberal politics divorces politics from life. Here is life with all it has to hold—its cultural, aesthetic, and artistic possibilities—and there is politics. That goes back to

John Locke. But in any crisis this hasn't worked. In any crisis people want what I call a fully furnished home. That is to say, politics must be integrated to the kind of healthy world of beauty and happiness that everyone really longs for. So aesthetics are always there. Now some of the fascist leaders were very well able to articulate this aesthetic longing as a part of mass participation, that is to say, in the way mass meetings were arranged. I remind you that the British ambassador thought the Nuremberg rallies were more beautiful than any ballet he had seen. Other admirers, like the French fascists, were terribly taken by the simplicity and beauty of the mise en scene. In one of these festivities let us remember that Speer took great pains using lights to darken the fat stomachs of the Gautleiters so that they all approximated the stereotypes. So there was a great deal here, especially in the speeches. What is important in a mass movement is rhythm, and Hitler's speeches had rhythms in which the people could join. This was true for D'Annunzio and for Mussolini as well. Now this is really what Brasillach and Jose Antonio Primo de Rivera[62] in Spain meant when they called all this poetic. They meant that it was aesthetic. The politics of beauty counts in mass movements, and the politics of beauty are based not only on liturgy but also on taking up, as all fascism did, this longing for vitalism, for elan, that you have with Bergson, Nietzsche, and so many at the turn of the century. It therefore becomes a mixture between beauty and this kind of elan which expresses itself in rhythm—bodily rhythm, speech rhythm, the ecstasy that expresses itself in a kind of poetry. Let us not forget that Nietzsche was above all a poet.

Ledeen: Why do you think that the poetics of revolution are the poetics of a right wing rather than a left wing revolution?

Mosse: Well again it's difficult for me to answer. But there's much too much rationalism and didacticism in socialism to have such flights into fancy; it does not confront this problem of irrationalism and rationalism, elan and vitalism. When Eisner made his revolution in Bavaria he topped it off with a meeting in the opera in tails and top hat and with speeches—speeches above all. The socialist movement was directed toward speeches because of their educational function.

Ledeen: Long speeches?

Mosse: Yes, longish speeches. Let me put it another way. The German Democratic Republic is publishing a great many of the early workers' plays dramas which are of the greatest importance, and there you can see that the dramatic form is always subjugated by didacticism.

Ledeen: They are always preaching?

Mosse: I would not say preaching. There are conversation and dialogue, but dialogues which lack any dramatic tension—which are rather expository. There is a famous play, for example, which in dialogue form gives you the essence of the theory of surplus-value. Many plays are that way. Fascism and the Right were not handicapped by an appeal to learning in this sense at all. They could go into discontinuities, into flights of fantasy and poetics provided they were always contained within the mass movement. It was in the end a phony elan—a substitute vitality as it were—because as D'Annunzio so rightly said, "Beauty means not only ecstasy, but above all every beauty has a principle of order." That he got, like everybody else, from Hegel. So we must say finally that such political liturgy appealed to the masses.

I always disliked the word propaganda. It's a very misleading word in this connection because propaganda means manipulation. But I believe fascist mass movements were in fact movements of consensus rather than of manipulation. What Professor De Felice said about Italy in this regard is totally correct: fascism gave people a feeling of participation, a feeling of experiencing a kind of preview of utopia which was more meaningful to most people than parliamentary government or speeches. Even today in our student movements in the U.S. they love to march to the capitol of the state (which is a classical building)—the speeches are not really very important even here because you know in advance what is going to be said. People participate through ritual. Political government has escaped them—it is too big, too impersonal, there is a crisis, they want a fully furnished house. All this appeals. I think we must not confuse it with propaganda which would be taking it too lightly.

Ledeen: Apropos of De Felice he said in that connection that the creation of the fascist consensus really represented a political revolution in Italian history because it was the first time a political movement had attempted to involve the masses, to gain the participation of the masses in the politics of the regime. Do you think the same is true for national socialism?

Mosse: No, no, it is not so because in Central and Western Europe things were different. There are mass movements—socialism is one—but there are also movements of the Right like that connected with Karl Lueger the Lord Mayor of Vienna, whom Hitler admired so much. And above all, of course, there are many precedents in France for that is where Le Bon got his theory of *The Crowd.* Le Bon got his ideas from observing the movement around General Boulanger[63] which everybody had thought was reactionary but

which modern studies have shown involved socialists
as well as conservatives. It was a kind of cross-class
crowd movement. So I would say that France
pioneered in this case and that the Boulangist movement was probably the first of what Le Bon calls the
"heterogeneous" crowd, which was a cross-class crowd.
We know that Hitler and Mussolini studied this, so
there is a definite connection from the French experience to the later fascist experience, and Gustav Le
Bon's work is the bridge. In Central and Western
Europe much more than in Italy, of course, you had
prior mass movements.

Perhaps I should come back at the end to something
I have already mentioned: that in fascism you always
have a dialectic, even between different myths. You
have apparently contradictory myths so that, for
example, Hitler was very fond of reading the German
popular author Karl May[64] who was a liberal in the
sense that he put forward in his novels about American
Indians ideas of toleration, piety, helping the oppressed, and avoiding force. Now one asks, why did Hitler
like to read this to his nephew—to finance out of his
own pocket the distribution of these novels to the
troops during World War II? The reason is that these
novels are also about middle-class morality. The Indians and the white man on the plains of North Dakota
observe all the so-called proprieties: they are clean cut,
they work, they're loyal, they celebrate religious festivals, all of that sort of thing. So the answer is perhaps
again, that in national socialism many people thought
that a Hitler was necessary in order that the fairy tale
could begin. So that though the fairy tale was said to
have already existed in the past, this was never per-
ceived as totally true because even when Hitler looked
at Wilhelminian Germany (or fin de siècle Austria) and
said these were good times, times when morality
reigned, they were never in reality like this at all. So

that in the end, of course, a fairy tale would reign—there would be a utopia that would presumably be better than what had existed before. It would be a breakthrough of the true Aryan spirit. I think we have to sum it up that way. I'm sure many people said that, well, it is too bad what is happening to the Jews, it is too bad that we're forbidden to read this or that, but, look, it is necessary so that we can live in the kind of happy, healthy, and clean-cut world that we desire. Of course Hitler played on these fantasies. Therefore, once more I come to something we have been discussing all along: that a unicausal explanation of this phenomenon will not do, that you have to bring in people and the desires and myths of people which are not always directly determined by their so-called objective class position. Usually people have false rather than true consciousness in this regard. As history is still made by people and based on people, certainly this has to be part of the historical dialectic. It seems to me very sterile to mouth slogans of class, capitalism, or reactionary without defining them in terms of their situation and without connecting them to the kind of world people want. In other words, these categories, useful though they are and investigated though they must be in detail, should be connected to the myths by which people live, to their attitudes of life. And these attitudes are never so crudely determined by the political and economic environment as some historians seem to believe. We must finally discard unmediated and positivist analyses for the examination of a mediated dialectic.

Chapter Seven

Ledeen: We've been talking about the fascist revolution, and yet the word fascist is very frequently applied to phenomena which are anything but revolutionary. Franco has been called a fascist, Salazar has been called a fascist, you would hardly call these two figures revolutionary.

Mosse: Well fascism has become a slogan, like liberalism or even socialism, but there is no greater mistake than to confuse fascist with reactionary. Modern scholarship is quite firm on that question. Let us take Franco first. Franco suppressed his fascist party, the Falange, because it was too revolutionary. Antonio Salazar, and let us add some others, Horthy, the dictator of Hungary between the wars and Antonescu, Hitler's dictator of Rumania; these were men who were, in fact, antifascists in this regard: that they hated revolution and thought in terms of traditional, inherited hierarchies. There was never an ideal of hierarchy of function not status for these men. They turned it around. Everything was hierarchy of status. Moreover, these people believed that as long as the traditional structures of state and church were intact, it didn't really matter much what people said or did. That is to say, they did not want to open a window on mens' hearts or heads, they did not want to control or organize all of life. What they were interested in was that the traditional structures remain intact (the traditional hierarchies as they had come down from the past) and that these hierarchies rest on three pillars: the traditional ruling classes, the church, and the army. As long as these were allied to and in fact controlled the government, everything was all right. This is quite different from fascism. In fact, they all tried to suppress their fascisms (except perhaps for Salazar who only had a tiny fascist movement). Moreover, it must be said of course, that all of them rejected ideas of race because the church was one of their pillars—and indeed, they proved rather friendly towards Jews in some respects, if only to oppose the fascists who were hostile.

Ledeen: Well let's not get carried away. Franco to a certain extent, yes, but one wouldn't call the Iron Guard friendly to Jews.

Mosse: That is not what I'm talking about. I'm talking about Antonescu.

Ledeen: Would you call Antonescu friendly to Jews?

Mosse: Well he did what Petain[65] did, he sacrificed some Jews in the case of Besarabia, but protected native Jews. In fact he stopped the deportation of Jews in Rumania, and Horthy tried to do this as well. Figures like Antonescu and Horthy were afraid of mass movements and the attack on law and order that might come with the Nazi Jewish deportations. This is why they opposed them as much as they could—they wanted no disturbance of tradition or hierarchies.

Ledeen: So one doesn't want to confuse fascism with pure reaction or authoritarian governments. I suppose you'd say the same about Pinochet in Chile, the Greek colonels, and so forth.

Mosse: These are traditional military dictatorships, though there exists a national socialist party that is in some way linked to the antisemitic military junta that rules Chile today.

Ledeen: I think that we ought to say a few things about revolution. We've used the term fascist revolution over and over again and, of course, when we used the term revolution we're not using it in the way that many people use the term today.

Mosse: I've already said before the kind of revolution it is—it's a revolution of the Right, it's a revolution not of function but of status, it's a revolution which doesn't change economic relationships except that it is not bound by any one economic theory, it can nationalize, it can ally itself with big industry and agriculture, it can do all sorts of things.

Ledeen: Or it can do nothing.

Mosse: Or it can do nothing. It can leave it alone, but it didn't or at least not in Germany. So it is a peculiar kind of revolution which comes from the end of the nineteenth century—for example the revolution of bourgeois youth against their parents—but which takes in expressionism in art and literature, etc. This is a revolution which all fascism, I believe, took up, and which was strengthened by the war. It is a revolution which wanted (what we've said so often before) a new man and which looked for vitality and action, but at the same time for the restoration of a system of traditional, middle-class morality; which looked to the nation or the race; and which thought that if you had a new attitude toward life, all social and economic problems would soon settle themselves.

Ledeen: Once you got the new man, he would settle them.

Mosse: Not only that. Once you got the regime in power, once the Aryans ruled and excluded the Jews things would be solved.

Ledeen: But what kind of social and economic tranformations, if any, did national socialism actually achieve in power?

Mosse: The only kind of economic and social tranformations which national socialism achieved in power were that it substituted a new ruling class for the old and that in many ways it substituted new men who did not come from the traditional ruling classes for those who had ruled in the Republic or in the Second Empire. It, of course, eliminated a part of the population gradually, not until after 1937—that is the important Jewish economic, social, and cultural segment. It was small in number—only some 500,000—but rather important. In reality that is the only transformation apart, of course, from what you might call its "New Deal" aspects—the use of public works to get rid of umemployment, the large-scale use of the new armament industry, and of course, as I said already, the beauty of work, the modernization of factories, the introduction into factories of new sanitary criteria, but not raising real wages. The real pay never rose, but that did not seem so important compared with the status and participation. In other words, workers might not get paid more, but now they could travel and go to the theater.

Ledeen: Fringe benefits.

Mosse: Not so fringe. Their leisure time was revolutionized. I would say that work was not revolutionized—the work process was improved only insofar as light and air were concerned—but what was revolutionized was the leisure process as it was in Italian fascism through *dopolavoro.* Moreover, we must not forget that national socialism did nationalize some industry and eventually controlled all industry. That is to say it is not true, as one always hears, that Krupp dictated to Hitler, but rather that Hitler dictated to Krupp. Eventually with the five-year plan Goering, as the commissioner, took over whole industries such as the steel industry which was in effect nationalized. So that you might say that the Nazis created in a kind of chaotic way a planned economy—planned with war production in mind.

Ledeen: Yes. A lot of people forgot about the nationalization or the Aryanization of these industries.

Mosse: Nationalization and Aryanization must not be confused. They are not necessarily related. The steel industry was nationalized. It became the Herman Goering Works, now called the Saltzgitter Steel Works belonging to the German federal government. Aryanization was not nationalization. It was very largely a transfer to other private, not national, enterprises.

Ledeen: But there was plenty of Aryanization and transfer to national enterprises—the Petchek Steel Works in Czechoslovakia, for instance.

Mosse: Correct. This was accomplished as part of the general steel nationalization. The Aryanization played into it, but I think we must distinguish between the two. So that we cannot say that national socialism continued the status quo. This is absolutely incorrect. Nor did it make a revolution in the tradition of Marxist or bolshevist revolution. It fell somewhere in between. The aim was always, as Hitler put it, "a revolution of the spirit" which became in the end the anti-Jewish revolution. A revolution must have a focus, but what the capitalists were to the Bolsheviks, the Jews were to Hitler. Perhaps that is the easiest way to put it.

Ledeen: This brings us now to the question of the limits of fascism—to whether or not one can speak of a fascist epoch or whether it's a phenomenon that exists above and beyond the period between World War I and II. You said at the very end of *The Nationalization of the Masses,* "this book deals with a past which to most men seems to have ended with the second world war. In reality, it is still contemporary history." What exactly did you mean by that? Do you think that national socialism is still alive?

Mosse: No, I do not think national socialism as such is still alive. I think we must distinguish two things: the reality of fascist regimes and the ideas and values which they annexed, such as mass politics and mass participation. I have said earlier that in any severe crisis, parliamentary government does not work very well and people long for a total attitude of life which integrates all their aesthetic, political, economic, and social desires. In such moments, therefore, political participation is again defined outside parliament and there is a longing for a kind of charismatic leadership. We have all seen that resurface (at least in America and Germany to a certain extent) in the student rebellions from '68 onwards with their emphasis on symbols, myths, processions, and an emerging leadership. They are antiliberal, antiparliamenarian, and to a certain extent antirational. That is, I think, what is lasting.

Ledeen: If we are talking about student movements, we can extend it to France and Italy and not just restrict it to Germany and America.

Mosse: Because I do not know much about France and Italy I do not want to talk about it, but I do know something about Germany and the United States in this regard.

Ledeen: Do you think that there's a contemporary fascist movement of the sort that you have written about? Do you see any signs of a renascent fascism any place?

Mosse: Well, we must now make a distinction again between fascism and national socialism. Which do you mean?

Ledeen: Why don't we take them one by one?

Mosse: National socialism is not reviving. There could be no national socialism without Adolf Hitler, and no leader with Hitler's peculiar combination of traits is even on the horizon. Those political parties in the federal republic which are always called new Nazi parties are in reality old line conservative parties, closer to the German National party in the Weimar Republic rather than the Nazis. I think this has something to do with the evolution of racism. I do not think racist ideas are dead. After Auschwitz there was a moratorium on racism as far as the Jews are concerned, but there was never a moratorium as far as blacks are concerned. However, that moratorium regarding the Jews was in my opinion lifted, first in France, which once more becomes the center of antisemitism during the Algerian war and its aftermath. I would say that there is very little racism in Germany now, but anti-Jewish racism still exists in Europe, fastening onto an old tradition. In Eastern Europe, of course, there is a thin line between the advocacy of complete assimilation and racism, and I think in some countries of Eastern Europe the traditional Marxist idea of complete assimilation has definite racist overtones. You can see this in their Jewish iconography,—in how Jews are pictured as the stereotype in some of their publications. So I would say that racism survived Auschwitz, greatly weakened for the Jews and the blacks (except in South Africa). Racism in Germany, however, is effectively gone and, since racism is the essence of national socialism I should say that there is no revival of national socialism in the offing, at least not in Germany. And since its history and tradition was in Central and Eastern Europe, I think we can say that there is no sign of a revival of national socialism anywhere.

Ledeen: What about neofascism?

Mosse: Well, neofascism has obviously revived in Italy. Fascism had one strength to it: it had no Auschwitz. It did not really have a concentration camp system like that in Germany. The terror was not as dense, if I can put it that way.

Ledeen: There were some camps, however . . .

Mosse: Yes, there were some camps, but nothing like the whole network which you had in Germany, so that it was possible to look back with a kind of nostalgia to Italian fascism. This was clearly not possible so far as national socialism was concerned, and so it was easier to take the bits and pieces which are at the basis of all fascism and try to reconstruct them on the model of

Italian fascism—the longing for a leader, camaraderie and a revolution of the Right; the mass movement and myth and symbol; the appeal to the mystical side of human nature.

Ledeen: Evidently, then, you do not agree with someone like James Gregor[66] who believes that fascism is the result of a crisis in a society at a certain moment of industrialization and modernization, and who therefore sees fascist-type regimes emerging today in North Africa and perhaps in some countries of Eastern Europe.

Mosse: Well, this is not only Gregor. Professor Hugh Seton-Watson[67] took a similar position at one point. I myself do not know enough about the Third World to make such a statement, except to say that it is true that Kwame Nkrumah[68] in Ghana had a political institute which accepted many parts of fascism or tried to adapt them to that situation. I am not sure myself how much one can really talk about fascism in an underdeveloped country. For fascism you need a modern state, a bureaucracy, a leader, as we have said again and again, who puts forward a myth in which everyone believes—something which is difficult in tribal societies—and who is a symbol of a nation. Not only do you need a modern nation, you also need a united nation and I'm not sure how united some of the Third World nations are.

Ledeen: Do you think you need a western nation? Do you think fascism is a western phenomenon?

Mosse: By "western" you mean all of Europe, including Eastern Europe, I take it?

Ledeen: Yes.

Mosse: In Eastern Europe there were fascist movements like the Iron Guard and the Arrow Cross, even if they were different in many respects from those in Central and Southern Europe and just as these differed among themselves. I think there were Europeanwide fascist movements in the 1920s and '30s. Now I am not an authority on the Third World; I do not know how much, let us say, Islam and the kind of tribal religions in Africa are a barrier to the secular religion of fascism. We must remember that fascism itself was in many ways a religion and didn't take kindly to other rival religions.

Ledeen: Do you see in the West today anything like a tendency for a new kind of fascism? People have spoken a lot, for example, about the possibility of an American fascism where there is no fascist tradition.

Mosse: There is no possibility whatsoever of an American fascism. To me this is a totally ridiculous and unhistorical point of view. First of all, we have made it quite clear that fascism could not work unless it could annex already present traditions, so if there are no traditions which can lead into fascism, there can be no fascism at the end either. Secondly, I said fascism must come in unified countries. America is a regional country, one of more or less coherent ethnic groups which would be almost impossible to unify. As such the United States lacks the first and most elementary prerequisite for fascism, namely an integrated nationalism.

Ledeen: And Western Europe today?

Mosse: Your question is asked from a liberal point of view. What you really mean is, "Is parliamentary government to go under?" Yes, parliamentary govern-

ment will go under in the first real crisis, as it has
always done. But what follows might be a people's
republic—a bolshevization of Europe—or you could
reassemble the bits and pieces of past fascism. At any
rate, if you look at Europe today, where are the Mus-
solinis or Hitlers? You cannot have national socialism
without Hitler, and certainly you need something like
Mussolini for Italian fascism. I do not see them on the
horizon, but an historian is never a good prophet.
Perhaps, I can sum it up in a little different way. I think
it is quite arid to speculate on history repeating itself
because history never does repeat itself; it is only bits
and pieces which are put together in a different way. I
would say what we face again is that there are certain
factors inherent or potential in modern nationalism,
the modern state and the view of man that we have
discussed, which might be reconstructed in an authoritarian way. But there is something else in fascism
that we must not lose sight of and which it really shares
with all ideologies: the urge to transform myth into
reality. Perhaps it is well to summarize in a proper
manner something we have said before. Repeatedly I
have made the point that you cannot understand fascism simply as an economic, social, or political
phenomenon and the reason is clear: fascism puts
forward a myth—the myth of a happy and healthy
world, the myth of the new man, the myth of race in
Germany—and then it tries to actualize this myth.
Fascism thinks in stereotypes and it tries to transform
stereotypes into reality as, to take an extreme situation,
the Nazis tried to do with the Jews in the concentration
camps. And indeed, together with that we must say
that fascism attempts to be a self-fulfilling prophecy.
The best example of this is Hitler saying that if the
Jews start another war, this will mean their extermination. So Hitler made this prophecy come true by starting the war himself, blaming the Jews, and then ex-

terminating them. Fascism is full of self-fulfilling prophecies. Now the frightening thing about all fascism is, in my opinion, this strong urge to transform an irrational myth and stereotypes into reality once it gets the means—and the means are the modern state—into its hands. However, all of this might be obsolete by now for a very simple reason: fascism, like all modern political theories, is essentially a theory of productivity. It distinguishes between those who produce and those who don't produce, between what the Nazis called "parasites" and "activists." But in the modern world any theory based on productivity may no longer work, because in a world of scarcity these modern political theories may be irrelevant and productivity can no longer be the main goal. In the new world of scarcity that is upon us all past political theories may find themselves very much out of date.

Notes

1. The Ullstein family owned the Ullstein Verlag, the biggest publishing house in pre-Hitler Germany. The best known newspaper of the family was the *Vossiche Zeitung*. After the Ullsteins emigrated, the name of the house was changed to Deutscher Verlag.

2. "Aryanization" made it possible for the Nazi leadership to change someone's racial status. Such special treatment was quite exceptional. Hitler himself never condoned this practice.

3. The *Sturmabteilung* (SA), or storm troops, were one of the paramilitary arms of the national socialist movement. Led for a time by the charismatic but highly eccentric Ernst Röhm, they were stripped of power on the so-called "night of the long knives," the purge of 30 June 1934.

4. G.M. Trevelyan, *A History of England* (London: Longmans, 1926).

5. H.G. Koenigsberger and G.L. Mosse, *Europe in the Sixteenth Century* (London: Longmans, 1968).

6. George L. Mosse, *The Culture of Western Europe: the Nineteenth and Twentieth Centuries*, 2nd ed. (Chicago: Rand McNally & Co., 1974).

7. George L. Mosse, *The Holy Pretence, a Study in Christianity and Reason of State from William Perkins to John Winthrop*, 2nd ed. New York: Howard Fertig, 1968).

8. George L. Mosse, *The Crisis of German Ideology* (New York: Grosset and Dunlap, 1964).

9. George L. Mosse, "The Mystical Origins of National Socialism" in *The Journal of the History of Ideas* (1959).

130

10. George L. Mosse, *The Nationalization of the Masses* (New York: Howard Fertig, 1975).

11. On January 11, 1923, the French occupied the Ruhr Valley which they announced was compensation for the German failure to make reparation payments as stipulated in the Versailles Treaty at the end of World War I.

12. Alois Hudal (1885-1963). Hudal was the German bishop in Rome at the German Institute of Santa Maria dell'Anima for many years. Violently anticommunist, he wrote *The Foundations of National Socialism* (1936) in an attempt to reconcile national socialism and the Catholic church.

13. The *Ermächtigungsgesetz* or Enabling Act (23 March 1933), passed immediately after the Reichstag fire, gave the government dictatorial powers until 1 April 1937. This act established the Nazi dictatorship.

14. For the "beauty of work" see Anson G. Rabinbach, "The Aesthetics of Production in the Third Reich," *Journal of Contemporary History* October 1976. Albert Speer (1905-), Hitler's architect and later Minister of Munitions, author of *Inside the Third Reich*, gave numerous lengthy interviews to George Mosse which are cited in *The Nationalization of the Masses*.

15. Renzo de Felice, *Fascism; an Informal Introduction* (New Brunswick: Transaction, 1977). For the concept of the "new fascist man" see also Michael A. Ledeen, "Fascist Social Policy" in Irving Louis Horowitz, ed., *The Use and Abuse of Social Science* (New Brunswick: Transaction, 1970).

16. Heinrich Himmler (1900-1945). Head of the SS, Himmler organized and carried out "the final solution," — the destruction of the European Jews. The *Schutzstaffel* (SS) — the "protection squads" — was created as Hitler's personal bodyguard. Starting with 250 men in 1929, it reached 210,000 in 1936, and became in effect the pretorian guard of Nazism following the downgrading of Röhm's SA in 1934.

17. *Lebensborn* was the not very successful Nazi program for the creation of a pure Aryan race. For this program and other aspects of Nazi racism see George L. Mosse, *Towards the Final Solution: The European Experience of Race* (New York: Howard Fertig, 1978).

18. Tim Mason, "Das Primat der Politik. Politik und Wirtschaft im Nationalsozialismus" in *Das Argument*, 41: 473-94.

19. Reinhard Kühnl, *Formen bürgerlicher Herrschaft: Liberalismus-Fascismus* (Hamburg, 1971).

20. Gustav Krupp von Bohlen und Halbach, the so-called king of munitions makers in Germany, head of the great arms factory in Essen. Fritz Thyssen was the head of the important German steel

trust, the Vereinigte Stahlwerke.

21. See Anson G. Rabinbach, "Toward a Marxist Theory of Fascism and National Socialism: A Report on Developments in West Germany" in *New German Critique* 3, Winter 1974.

22. See George L. Mosse, "The German Socialists and the Jewish Question during the Weimar Republic" in *Yearbook of the Leo Baeck Institute* 4, 1971.

23. Ernst Nolte, *Der Faschismus in seiner Epoche* (Munich, 1963); *Die Krise des liberalen Systems und die Faschistichen Bewegungen* (Munich, 1968).

24. See George L. Mosse, "The Genesis of Fascism," in Laqueur and Mosse eds. *International Fascism* (New York: Harper Torchbooks, 1966).

25. Mosse, *The Nationalization of the Masses,* op cit., 76-77.

26. Walter Rathenau (1887-1922), industrialist and liberal German politician, Minister of Reconstruction and Foreign Minister in the early years of the Weimar Republic. He was assassinated by ultranationalists in 1922.

27. Two of the leaders of the *Freikorps.*

28. Gustave Le Bon, *Psychologie des Foules* (Paris, 1895).

29. See Rudolph Binion and others, "New Findings on Hitler and Germany: a Symposium," *History of Childhood Quarterly,* Fall 1973.

30. Dietrich Eckardt (1868-1923), journalist and author, close friend of Hitler. He was the editor of the journal *Auf gut Deutsch* which was important in the evolution of *völkisch* thought and then editor of the *Völkischer Beobachter,* the official Nazi newspaper.

31. *Lebensraum*—literally, "living space"—indicated the desire of the Germans to expand into Central Europe in order to establish an autarchic economic system. The concept and the goal were clearly delineated with the founding of a united Germany in 1871.

32. From the word *volk,* or "people." In the German cultural context of the nineteenth century the word *volk* indicated all the elements—historic, cultural, traditional, mystical—that went into the formation of the so-called German "character."

33. The Hungarian fascist movement.

34. For Rumanian fascism, popularly known as the Iron Guard, see Eugen Weber, *Varieties of Fascism* (New York, 1960), and "The Men of the Archangel" in Laqueur and Mosse eds., *International Fascism.*

35. Walter Laqueur, *Young Germany* (New York, 1962).

36. For the phenomenon of the youth movement see Walter Laqueur, *Young Germany,* op cit.,; Michael A. Ledeen, "Fascism and the Generation Gap" in *European Studies Review* (London, 1971)

and *Universal Fascism* (New York, 1971).

37. *The Nationalization of the Masses,* op. cit., 177 ff.

38. Renzo de Felice, *Mussolini e Hitler* (Florence, 1975).

39. Hannah Arendt, *Eichmann in Jerusalem* (New York, 1963).

40. *The Diary of Anne Frank.*

41. Bruno Bettelheim, *The Informed Heart* (Glencoe, 1960).

42. Reinhard Heydrich (1904-1942). Heydrich was Chief of the SD, the Security Police which within the SS was, among other matters, in charge of the extermination of the Jews.

43. Hannah Arendt, *The Origins of Totalitarianism* (New York, 1951).

44. On the night of 10 November 1938 the Nazis launched a violent attack on Jewish property, stores, synagogues, etc.

45. See A.J.P. Taylor, *The Origins of the Second World War* (London, 1961).

46. Alfred Rosenberg (1893-1946). Nazi ideologue, Rosenberg was the author of *The Myth of the Twentieth Century* which, along with Hitler's *Mein Kampf,* was one of the official texts of Nazism.

47. General Heinz Guderian (1888-1955) was the creator and leader of the famed *Panzer* tank divisions.

48. Gustav Landauer (1870-1919), the German socialist and anarchist, was a leader of the Bavarian revolution of 1919.

49. Robert Brasillach (1900-1945), novelist and French fascist, collaborated with the Nazis during the occupation of France.

50. Pierre Joseph Proudhon (1809-1865), French socialist and anarchist; Edouard Drumont (1844-1917), author of *La France Juive* (1886) and editor of *Libre Parole,* was the leading French anti-semite of his time and an important national socialist.

51. Christian de La Mazière, *The Captive Dreamer* (New York: Saturday Review Press, 1972).

52. See Renzo de Felice, *Fascism,* op cit.

53. Jacob L. Talmon, *The Origins of Totalitarian Democracy* (London, 1952).

54. Peter Gay, *The Enlightenment* Vol. 1 (New York: Alfred A. Knopf, 1966), Vol. 2 (1969); for the underside of the Enlightenment see George L. Mosse, *Towards the Final Solution,* Chapter 1.

55. Renzo de Felice, *Mussolini il duce, I, gli anni del consenso (1929-1936)* (Turin, 1974).

56. On Farinacci, see Ugoberto Alfassio Grimaldi and Gherardo Bozzetti, *Farinacci; il più fascista* (Milan, 1972).

57. Giovanni Preziosi (1881-1945). Unfrocked priest, then nationalist journalist, then fascist. During the last phase of Italian fascism—the days of the Republic of Salò—he was in charge of "racial policies."

58. Julius Evola (1898-1974). Painter, philosopher, and writer. Traditionalist, Spenglerian mystic, spiritualist racist. Author, among many other works, of *Note sul Terzo Reich* (Milan, 1964).

59. Herder's theories on the origins of European languages was influential in many national liberation movements during, the nineteenth century.

60. Robert Koehl, "The Neofeudal Aspects of National Socialism" in *American Journal of Economics and Sociology,* January 1959.

61. Unpublished manuscript by Walter Dean Burnham of the Massachusetts Institute of Technology.

62. Jose Antonio Primo de Rivera (1903-1936). Leader of the Falangist movement in Spain, Primo de Rivera was executed by the republicans in 1936.

63. Georges Ernst Jean Marie Boulanger (1837-1891). Leader of a nationalist movement which carried his name, Boulanger advocated the revision of the Constitution of 1875.

64. Karl May (1842-1912). May was the author of numerous best sellers about life on the American frontier and in Persia.

65. Henri Philippe Pétain (1856-1951). Pétain was the head of the Vichy government during the German occupation of France.

66. James Gregor, *The Ideology of Fascism* (New York, 1969).

67. Hugh Seton-Watson, "Fascism Right and Left" in Laqueur and Mosse, *International Fascism,* op. cit.

68. Kwame Nkrumah (1909-1972). Nkrumah was the leader of the Convention People's party and first President of the Republic of Ghana, which was overthrown in 1966.